D1479439

THE ULTIMATE HISTORY OF Ferrari

This is a Parragon Publishing Book
First published in 2002

Parragon Publishing
Queen Street House
4 Queen Street
Bath BA1 1HE, UK

ISBN: 0-75258-873-7

A copy of the CIP data for this book is available from the British Library upon request.

The rights of Brian Laban to be identified as the author of this work have been asserted in accordance with Section 77 of the Copyright, Designs and Patents Act of 1988.

Created by Essential Books

Printed and bound in China

Photographic and Picture credits

Automobili Lamborghini 59 (bottom left), 66 (middle), 110
Ferrari UK 6, 123, 124, 125, 128, 129, 130 (top left), 131, 132, 133, 134 (top), 135, 187 (main and bottom right)
Ford Motor Company 150 (middle)
The GP Library 138,139, 141 (top and bottom right), 144 main, 145,146,147, 148 (main), 149 (main), 151, 152 (right), 153 (main), 154, 155, 158, 159, 161, 162, 163, 166, 168, 171, 172, 173 (left), 174, 175, 176, 177, 179 (left), 180, 181,182 (top left and top right), 183, 184, 185 (left), 186, 191 (top), 192.
Mercedes-Benz 30 (middle)
Jaguar Diamler Heritage Trust 30 (bottom)
Porsche Cars 1 05
Grant Scott 185 (details on right)

Other pictures © Neill Bruce's Automobile Photolibrary by:
Tony Bader 30 (top)
Geoffrey Goddard 15, 73, 74, 86 (bottom right), 153(right top and botom details), 170, 182 (bottom), 190
Christian Gozenbach 122 (main)
Bengt Holm 49 (top), 108 (bottom), 109 (main)
Stefan Lüscher 130 (bottom left)

All other photographs and pictures © Neill Bruce's Automobile Photolibrary, with the exception of the following, which are manufacturer's press pictures supplied from The Peter Roberts Collection c/o Neill Bruce: 8-9, 10, 11, 12, 13, 14 top, 16, 17, 18, 39, 58, 65 (b/w), 66 (bottom), 72 bottom, 86 (bottom left), 94 (top left), 96 (bottom) 97 (top right), 107(top right), 108 (top), 117, 118 (top), 122 (top), 142 (top), 178

Neill Bruce gives special thanks to Duncan Hamilton Ltd. for making so many superb cars available.

THE ULTIMATE HISTORY OF Ferrari

BRIAN LABAN

p

2000 Ferrari Rossa concept car built by Pininfarina to mark their 70th anniversary

Contents

2002 Ferrari 575 Maranello

The story of Ferrari has probably been told more often than the story of any other automobile company in history, but the reason it has been told so often is that the subject is genuinely so fascinating, and open to so many different approaches. The secret of writing something more than just another Ferrari book is to tell the story well, to tell it in as much detail as space allows, and to tell it not only with affection but also with a critical eye. That is what *The Ultimate History of Ferrari* sets out to do, from Ferrari's roots to the present day, on road and track.

It looks first at what shaped and motivated Enzo Ferrari, the man—from long before his name ever appeared on an automobile of his own. It looks at his family background, his brief career as a racing driver, and his longer-lasting success as a team manager with Alfa Romeo. It looks at the origins of the Prancing Horse emblem, at the models Enzo Ferrari created for the road, and the models he created for motor sport—not only in Grand Prix and sportscar racing but for every level of motor sport from hillclimbs to Indianapolis. It looks at the development of the company as well as the machinery, at the designers, at the autos that were Ferrari in everything but name, and at Enzo Ferrari's often controversial style of combining all the diverse elements that make Ferrari unique and intriguing.

It looks at the ups and the downs. Ferrari has made glorious automobiles but has also made less-than-perfect ones, has dominated world motor racing but has also gone through nightmare periods when it couldn't come close to winning. But always, Ferrari has bounced back.

Throughout his lifetime, Enzo Ferrari famously did things his own way, and when arguing with the establishment (which he did for most of his life) he usually had his own way too. He was full of contradictions. He was a tough man to deal with but in other ways he was unexpectedly sentimental; he was controversial but often deeply conservative; and he was reclusive but he was without doubt one of the giants of motoring history. During his lifetime, the automobiles that the Ferrari company built and raced always had the stamp of Enzo Ferrari's greatness. After his death, Ferraris are unarguably still great, and in motor sport Ferrari is once again on top of the world. This is the story, simply told, of what created the legend.

Ferrari before Ferrari

In the galaxy of motoring superstars, no star burns brighter than Ferrari—maker of many of the world's greatest supercars, motor sporting giant, bearer of perhaps the most famous emblem in the motoring world. For more than half a century, Ferrari, the automobile, has been an icon. But long before Ferrari the automobile there was Ferrari the man, and more than a decade after his death, the legend of Enzo Ferrari burns as brightly as ever—a strange mixture of arrogance, sentimentality, unshakable stubbornness and, not least, an aura of mystery in which Ferrari himself clearly revelled.

Birth of an individualist

It's clear that Enzo Ferrari wasn't born to have an ordinary life. From the beginning, his story is spiced with drama—even in the story of his birth. He was actually born on February 18 1898 in Modena in northern Italy, but in the depths of winter the heavy snowfall meant his father couldn't immediately reach the local register office to record the event. Thus the baby's arrival was not formally registered until two days later, and ever after February 20 1898 was listed as Enzo Anselmo Ferrari's official birthdate.

He came to relish being the ultimate individualist, and it was obvious early on that Ferrari was a very ambitious young man indeed. As Ferrari the auto maker and motor sporting giant, the man's reputation eventually grew almost to rival that of the aristocracy, but his true family background was comfortable rather than privileged. His mother was originally from the city of Forlì, south of Ravenna on the Italian Adriatic coast. His father, Alfredo senior, hailed from Carpi, some eight miles north of Modena, and was a metalworker with his own modest business based in a workshop alongside the family house on the outskirts of Modena. He had profitable contracts with the state railroad company and, according to Enzo's memoirs and depending on

Previous page *Maestro Tazio Nuvolari masters the Scuderia Ferrari Alfa Romeo Tipo 12c, 1937*

Right *Monza Race Track, August 1923, from left to right, front row: Giorgio Rimini, Nicola Romeo (Alfa Romeo) and Enzo Ferrari, seated*

how much work was to hand, he employed as many as thirty laborers, but otherwise he ran everything himself, from designing to selling.

Enzo's elder brother, Alfredo junior, had two years on him and when they were young the two of them shared a room above their father's workshop. They kept homing pigeons and flew them in competitions, but they had quite different ambitions, in Enzo's case strangely at odds with what his life eventually held. Their father wanted both boys to become engineers but, formally at least, Enzo never did. While Alfredo was an enthusiastic pupil at the local school, Enzo hated studying and would have preferred to start working, but not with his hands. In his own words, "I think I should make it clear right away that my boyhood ambitions, in chronological order, were to be an opera singer, a sports writer, and lastly a racing driver."

He achieved two out of three; the singing career eluded him. As a student, though, he was keen on all kinds of sports, from track and field to gymnastics, fencing, and skating. The motor racing interlude came later, but in his mid-teens he wrote reports on local soccer matches for the *Gazzetta dello Sport* newspaper, and whatever his level of achievement later he was always proud of the fact that he had done that.

The fulfillment of the third of Ferrari's boyhood ambitions began early. His father was wealthy enough to be one of the first people in Modena to own an automobile, when such things were rare in rural Italy. He also added a motor repair works to his metalworking business, and Enzo sometimes helped in the workshops. While still reluctant to study engineering at school, he was obviously fascinated by the automobile, and by the time he was thirteen he was learning to drive. In September 1908, when he was ten, his father had taken him to nearby Bologna, where they saw Felice Nazzaro's Fiat winning the Coppa Florio road race. From then on, Enzo knew that motor sport would play some part in his future.

Above *Italian troops at the Alpine front, 1916. Enzo Ferrari was conscripted into the army in 1917 and attached to the Val Seriana detachment of the Third Mountain Artillery as a blacksmith*

War and the young racer

First he had to make his way in the world following the deaths of both his father and his brother within a few months of each other in 1916: Alfredo junior from "a malady caught while doing voluntary military service," Alfredo senior from pneumonia. As Enzo wrote later, "I found myself quite alone, and at a turning point in my life."

In 1917 he was conscripted into the army and pitched into World War One. With his family metalworking background he was sent to the Val Seriana detachment of the Third Mountain Artillery as a blacksmith, shoeing mules. But he was dogged by quite serious ill health and spent much of his service career in and out of various hospitals, in Brescia, in Baraccano and finally in Bologna. After many months of nursing and repeated surgery, Ferrari was discharged in 1918. He had no qualifications, no family business to fall back on, and apparently very few prospects.

His letter of introduction from the army failed to impress Fiat, but he did find work in a more modest branch of the auto industry with a Bolognese engineer called Giovanni, who was catering for the small post-war civilian market by stripping and rebuilding surplus light military vehicles. Part of Ferrari's job was to drive the rebuilt chassis from Turin to Milan, where they were rebodied—and that led indirectly to the next phase in his racing ambitions.

Through his delivery job, or more accurately through drinking in various Milanese bars between delivery jobs, Ferrari met many people who had previously been involved with racing—

***Right** 1914 Fiat trucks, the sort of vehicles that may well have been converted to civilian use post-war*

not least the great Felice Nazzaro, winner of the first race Enzo had ever watched. He also met Ugo Sivocci, who worked for Costruzioni Meccaniche Nazionale (CMN), a company which, like Ferrari's employer, was converting military vehicles for civilian use. CMN, however, already had plans to build more sporting machines, and Sivocci was both their test driver and a racing driver. Soon, Sivocci introduced Ferrari to CMN, and Ferrari too became a test driver for them.

It was the final step towards his real goal, and on October 5 1919 at the Parma Poggio di Bercetta hillclimb, driving a stripped CMN carrying the competition number 29, Enzo Ferrari became a racing driver. He took fourth place in the 3-liter class, some way behind the outright winner, Antonio Ascari in a 1914 GP Fiat.

The following month saw Ferrari and Sivocci competing with improved CMNs in the Targa Florio, the punishing Sicilian road race first run in 1906 when it was won by Alessandro Cagno's Itala, although they very nearly didn't make it to the start line. As they drove their open-topped machines, the story goes, through the remote and wintry Abruzzi mountains on their way to the race, Ferrari and Sivocci were attacked by wolves, and survived only because Ferrari was carrying a revolver under his seat cushion. A few shots from that, and the happy arrival on the scene of a group of road gangers armed with torches and guns, put the wolves to flight.

In this race, the first in Europe after the war, Enzo set off as the first of 24 starters. After four laps of the 67-mile Medium Madonie circuit, Sivocci finished seventh and Ferrari ninth, but many hours behind the winner, André Boillot. Naturally, Ferrari's race was far from straightforward. On the first lap his gas tank worked loose and he lost 40 minutes repairing the broken strap. That saw him restart way down, but near the end of the race, as he was making up some time, worse was to come. As Ferrari told the story himself, entering Campofelice he was stopped by three policemen standing in the middle of the track and told that he could not continue until the president of Italy had finished the speech he was delivering just along the road. The speech dragged on for a long time, and even when it was over Ferrari was not allowed to pass the limousine which drove the president slowly away. By the time he reached the finish line the timekeepers and spectators had left. His time was recorded by a man with an alarm clock. Technically he was a non-finisher, but after words with Vincenzino Florio himself, he was classified ninth.

Boillot's story, incidentally, would also have been worthy of Ferrari. Approaching the finish, he spun his Peugeot and crossed the line going backwards, resulting in him being sent back to the point where he had spun in order to finish again, the right way round.

Alfa Romeo and the P2

A year later, in November 1920, Ferrari was back at the Targa Florio with a new mount, and considerably more success. Driving for his new employer Alfa Romeo, he finished second to Meregalli's Nazzaro, and thus began a long and successful association with the marque from Milan. In 1921 he was second in the Circuit of Mugello, and in 1924 he won both the Coppa Acerbo and the Circuit of Polesine. In his own words, in the Coppa Acerbo "I finally made my name as a driver." Up against the all-conquering Mercedes squad, he was team-mate to the legendary Giuseppe Campari, who was driving the glorious Alfa P2 in one of its earliest races. Coincidentally, Ferrari's riding mechanic was Campari's cousin, Siena, and the two of them had been instructed that if they were leading at the start of the race and Campari's much faster P2 came up behind, they should let it pass, to take the fight to the Mercedes. It never did come up behind them. Campari had to retire early in the race, but he hid his car down a side road so that the Mercedes drivers would not know he had gone. Enzo became worried when Campari didn't materialize and slowed down to allow his compatriot to catch him and overtake; instead, the Mercedes of Bonmartini and Masetti came into view and began to bear down on him. Siena shouted at Enzo to keep them behind: "Keep going! Keep going, we're going to win—to win!" And they did.

Above *1914 GP Fiat*

Below *Antonio Ascari in his Fiat at the Parma Poggio di Bercetta hillclimb, October 1919*

Right The Alfa line-up for the 1920 Targa Florio. Drivers Campari, Ramponi and Ferrari (in middle car). Ferrari finished second

The Prancing Horse

Ferrari's emblem is probably the most famous motoring badge in the world, and the black prancing horse on the yellow shield has a story of its own, dating back to Enzo Ferrari's days as a racing driver.

On June 17 1923 Ferrari won the Circuito del Savio driving a 3-liter Alfa Romeo for the works team. The race was run on a road circuit near Ravenna, and Enzo's win was one of the best of his short career, during which he won about a dozen races in all. The Circuito del Savio, like most of them, wasn't hugely important, but Ferrari won well against strong opposition. He also set a new lap record, but the race goes down in Ferrari history for something much more important.

In the crowd was a local aristocrat, Count Enrico Baracca, and after the race Baracca was among those who congratulated Ferrari. He also invited Enzo to visit him and his wife, the Countess Paolina Baracca, at their home on the family estate near Ravenna.

The Baraccas were the parents of Francesco Baracca, Italy's top-scoring fighter ace in World War One. Francesco was born in 1888. In 1907, against his parents' wishes, he enrolled in the military academy in Modena, Enzo's home town, and in 1912 joined the

cavalry, but three years later moved to France to train as a pilot in the earliest days of military flying. Within a few weeks he had qualified as a star pupil, and went on to become an instructor.

When Italy entered the war in 1915, Baracca became a fighter pilot. He claimed his first victim in April the following year, and by the middle of 1918 he had taken his score to 34 kills. He had also survived his own airplane being hit several times, and was even forced down on one occasion. Among his many honors for bravery, Baracca was awarded Italy's highest, the Gold Medal for Military Valour. In November 1916 he was dubbed a Knight of the Air. Perhaps recalling his cavalry days, he added a crest, like knights of old, to the side of his airplane. It was a black prancing horse, the Cavallino Rampante, on a white background.

On June 19 1918 Baracca was in his SPAD fighter flying over the Austrian front when he was hit in the head by a single bullet, probably fired from the ground. Killed instantly, he crashed behind enemy lines, but in an act of chivalry his emblem was cut from his airplane and returned to his parents.

Which was why, five years later, Ferrari was invited to the Baraccas' home. The Countess dedicated her son's prancing horse symbol to the young racing driver from Modena, to bring luck to his career. The gesture may have been prompted as a result of the Modena connection, or perhaps because Enzo's older brother Alfredo had died while serving with Baracca's squadron earlier in the war. Either way, Ferrari accepted it as a great honor. He replaced the white background with a yellow shield, representing the civic color of Modena, and for the rest of his life he accorded Baracca's badge the utmost dignity, placing it on the racing models of Scuderia Ferrari and on all of Ferrari's greatest road autos.

***Left** c. 1924 Alfa Romeo P2 and **above** engine detail*

In between, in 1923, he won the Circuito del Savio in Ravenna, for which the parents of the wartime flying hero Francesco Baracca awarded Ferrari the emblem that was on his airplane when he was shot down and killed—a black prancing horse, which Ferrari placed on a yellow shield, honoring the color of Modena's flag (see box opposite).

These results suggested Ferrari showed some promise, and his own assessment was "I don't think I did too badly as a racing driver." But perversely, almost as soon as he had achieved that particular ambition he began to find himself attracted to what he had so stubbornly resisted at school and home—the engineering side of things.

It may have been a convenient way to stay close to the sport, because just as it had plagued his brief time in the army, ill health was already affecting Ferrari's career as a driver. In 1924 he should have driven one of the four works Alfa P2s in the Lyons Grand Prix, but he withdrew before the start. It has been suggested that it was a nervous breakdown, or at best a reaction to the death of his friend Sivocci in a practice accident before the 1923 Italian GP. Either way, it was the beginning of another new and pivotal phase in his life as Enzo Ferrari began to steer Alfa's race-engineering fortunes.

He finally, officially, retired as a driver in January 1932, after the birth of his son Dino. In reality he had already become far more a team manager than a driver. He still wasn't an engineer himself, and never claimed to be, but he had discovered an unerring facility for spotting talent. And one by one he began to bring legendary designers to Alfa's racing department. First came Luigi Bazzi, late of Fiat; then, at Bazzi's suggestion, the man who turned out to be the greatest of them all, Bazzi's former colleague from Fiat, the young Vittorio Jano. Between them, and with Enzo Ferrari increasingly taking control of the racing program, Alfa began to forge ahead. With the demise of Fiat as a major force in top-level motor sport after 1924, Alfa became the dominant manufacturer.

Led by Ferrari, the team developed the P1 and created the P2. The supercharged straight-eight P2 was one of the greatest racing machines of all time, and won first time out, for Campari in the 1924 French Grand Prix at Lyons—Ferrari failed to compete, of course—prior to that momentous Coppa Acerbo win. Later in 1924 Ascari's P2 won the Italian Grand Prix at Monza, and in 1925 the P2s gained the title of World Champion for Alfa, although Antonio Ascari was killed while the team was leading the French Grand Prix at Montlhéry.

Alfa's reign at the top of the motor racing world continued for most of the 1920s, mainly dominated by Jano's supercharged models. And through the whole decade Ferrari was at the heart of this, until a change of commercial fortunes for Alfa set up the next big move.

The break with Alfa

In December 1929 Ferrari officially left Alfa's employment, to resurface as head of a new Alfa racing team. In most respects it remained a works effort, but given Alfa's commercial problems the racing organization was diplomatically distanced from the auto-building side of the company. It was called Scuderia Ferrari, and for its emblem it had Baracca's black prancing horse on a yellow shield.

Scuderia Ferrari wasn't based in Milan but in Ferrari's home town, Modena. Its role was to run both its own automobiles, and those for the best of Alfa's private customers. Very soon, its "own" drivers included some of the best in the world, headed by the likes of Tazio Nuvolari, Giuseppe Campari, Louis Chiron, Guy Moll, Luigi Fagioli and Achille Varzi, among others. With a succession of increasingly brilliant cars, Alfa under Ferrari continued to win everything worth winning, from Grands Prix to the Targa Florio, the Mille Miglia and Le Mans. Then, in 1933, Alfa was nationalized and Scuderia Ferrari became even more officially responsible for Alfa's racing than it had been to date.

After a brief lull while things were reorganized, it was business as usual, the victories continuing to pile up, at least until the first appearances of the mighty, government-backed German Grand Prix teams began to turn the Alfa tide in the mid-1930s. For a while, the genius of Nuvolari could still overcome the sheer power of the Mercedes and Auto Unions, but by 1937 they were outclassed.

That year, Ferrari planned a new Grand Prix machine—according to him it was his own

Right *Antonio Ascari at the European Grand Prix at Spa, Belgium, 1925*

Below *Achille Varzi prepares his Alfa for the start in the 1930 Targa Florio*

Above Tazio Nuvolari (in leather helmet) with his arm around an Alfa Romeo

Left Guy Moll in a Scuderia Ferrari automobile at the Monaco Grand Prix, 1934

Auto Avio Costruzione and the 815

When Enzo Ferrari set up Auto Avio Costruzione after leaving Alfa Romeo in 1939 he may well have intended to honor the terms of their parting, which included a four-year embargo on Ferrari building an automobile under his own name to compete against Alfa in motor sport. With the advent of World War Two, however, that turned out to be a largely meaningless restriction, but even given the circumstances Ferrari didn't manage to stick by the letter of the agreement.

Auto Avio Costruzione was set up as an engineering and design consultancy, and considering that Ferrari's early employees included people like the brilliant engineer Luigi Bazzi, there was little doubt that Enzo's main interests were going to be in automobiles. Indeed, although the war saw the company building many other things, Ferrari's mind was never far away from motor sport.

In April 1940, before Italy entered the war, a version of the Mille Miglia (sometimes known as the Brescia Grand Prix) was run over six circuits of a triangular course linking Brescia, Mantua and Verona—the last race of the pre-war years. The only entries were from Germany and Italy; a BMW won, an Alfa Romeo came second. Also involved were two newcomers, two small sportscars from Auto Avio Costruzione built by Enzo Ferrari and called 815s.

The 815 was designed by former Alfa man Alberto Massimino and built for Fiat racer Marquis Lotario Rangoni Machiavelli after Fiat offered cash prizes for any class winner using Fiat components. The 815 engine used parts from two four-cylinder pushrod-valve Fiat engines in a special in-line eight-cylinder block. In its straight-eight layout it was like the 158 Massimino and Colombo had designed for Ferrari, and which became Alfa's virtually unbeatable "Alfetta" Grand Prix machine. The 815's unique block was topped by a one-piece cylinder head created by joining two Fiat four-cylinder heads, fed by four single-choke Weber carburetors—enough to give the 815 a maximum speed comfortably over 100mph. The cars carried two-seater spyder bodies with modern flared-fender lines over a Fiat-based chassis with independent front suspension, a live rear axle, drum brakes and wire wheels.

They made a promising debut, one car driven by Machiavelli, the other by Alberto Ascari, son of Alfa's legendary champion Antonio. Ascari was running away from the 1.5-liter opposition when he experienced engine problems. Then Machiavelli built up a huge class lead until he too had engine problems virtually within sight of the finish.

Ferrari blamed over-hasty preparation, but he must have been quite pleased with their obvious potential. Had the war not interrupted he would certainly have developed them further; instead, only one of them ever raced again, just once, at Pescara in 1948. And in that race it sat on the grid alongside the first real Ferrari.

***Top** The Scuderia Ferrari Alfa Romeos line up in 1936*

project—designed by a new Alfa engineer, Gioacchino Colombo, to be built in Modena. Then in 1938, faced with the might of the state-sponsored German Grand Prix teams from Auto Union and Mercedes, Alfa took the plunge back into Grand Prix racing under its own name. As Ferrari explains it, they did so by buying his racecar project from him. In the few remaining races in the late 1930s, they ran the machine as a "voiturette," one rung down from the Grand Prix class. But after the interruption of World War Two they went back to Ferrari's racers, and the four machines already under construction plus four more built later became some of the most successful Grand Prix racing models ever, the Alfa Romeo 158.

For a while in 1938, Alfa brought Enzo Ferrari back into the fold, as racing manager for what was now called Alfa Corse. Within months, however, it was clear that Enzo was far from comfortable with the new arrangement. He was by now a major figure in world motor sport, already a man who liked to have his own way. He didn't have much time for anyone he didn't genuinely respect, and back at Alfa he was clearly far from happy to be working with some of the people Alfa had in place.

In particular, he really couldn't come to terms with the director of Alfa's new "racing division," Wilfredo Ricart, a Spanish engineer who seems to have been pretty much on a par with Ferrari when it came to sheer arrogance. As Ferrari himself told the story, the eccentric Ricart (who had in effect replaced Enzo's earlier protégé Vittorio Jano) used to wear shoes with unusually thick India-rubber soles. When Ferrari asked him why, he replied that the brain of a great engineer "should not be jolted by the inequalities of the ground and consequently needed to be carefully sprung." He really wasn't Ferrari's type, and having failed to have him pushed into the background, Enzo finally broke his links with his old firm. As he wrote later, "I left with hardly any hard feelings, but sadly, all the same . . . I came to the conclusion that to spend a lifetime with one company is a mistake for anyone who wants to learn. To do that, one has to move around, and to do other things."

For Ferrari, "other things" were still centered on motor racing, but as part of the severance deal from Alfa there would be a four-year period when Enzo would not be allowed to go racing again under his own name, or in direct competition with his old company.

He left with a reasonable financial settlement and a small group of colleagues, the most important among them Luigi Bazzi. He immediately set up Auto Avio Costruzione, a design and engineering consultancy, in Modena (see box on p. 17). And whatever the terms of his agreement with Alfa about not racing against them for the next four years, he didn't show any serious signs of sticking to them.

By 1940 he had produced his first cars—Ferraris in everything but name. They were two small sportscars, which he entered in that year's Mille Miglia—a race run some time after war had broken out and won by BMW against modest German and Italian opposition. The cars were Fiat-based with 1.5-liter eight-cylinder engines, from which they took their name: 815, for eight cylinders and 1.5 liters, a numbering system Ferrari would return to much later as an auto builder in his own right. Both 815s led their class, both retired.

If Alfa felt inclined to protest against Ferrari's apparent disregard for their agreement, it wasn't the most important problem either of them faced as World War Two moved into full swing.

Left *1947 Alfa Romeo Tipo 158/47*

The First Generation

Through the first half of the 1940s, after he had parted company with Alfa Romeo, Ferrari had no more opportunity to play around with motor racing or fast cars than the rest of the world, locked as it was in the terrible conflict of World War Two. But even while he was involved in the war effort, Ferrari never stopped dreaming, and when the war ended and Europe struggled back to some kind of normality, the agreement restricting Enzo Ferrari from going racing under his own name and building his own automobiles to race with was long expired. What's more, Ferrari's ambition was as keen as ever, and by 1946 he was ready to fulfill it.

The 125s and 166s

He'd already bent the rules, of course, with the 815 racers built by Auto Avio Costruzione, and Enzo Ferrari had started as he meant to go on. In 1943 he'd moved his base from Modena to nearby Maranello, a medium-sized town about twenty miles west of Bologna, capital of the Emilia Romagna region of northern Italy. During the war, Auto Avio had grown quite large, working mainly for the military, building mechanical equipment, even making small aero engines, and employing more than a hundred people. The company had survived despite being bombed more than once after its move to Maranello, late in 1944 and early in 1945, and all the time Enzo was planning his future as a maker and racer of Ferraris.

Italy itself hadn't come out of the war too well—defeated, near bankrupt and in political chaos. But amazingly, Ferrari planned to launch his career as an auto builder with a big flourish. He wasn't the man to start with the sort of modest product the market might have expected at a time when money and materials were still short. He had plans to build Grand Prix cars, racing sportscars, and sportscars for the road—all of them sophisticated and expensive. He didn't need a huge number of customers, just the right ones. Starting a pattern that was to last for decades, the customer cars would be built mainly to finance the racing cars—the one thing Enzo Ferrari really lived for. And in the early days, the customer cars were sure to have racing blood coursing through them anyway.

The company was still called Auto Avio Costruzione, and would be for many years until it was reorganized as the Società Esercizio Fabbriche Automobili e Corse, or SEFAC, in 1960, but the automobiles it built were now bona fide Ferraris. Having been announced late in 1946, the first of them debuted in March 1947. It was labeled the 125, continuing the tradition begun with the 815s of numbering according to the capacity of a single cylinder. In all it had a dozen cylinders for an overall capacity of 1.5 liters. Its jewel of an engine was designed by Gioacchino

Previous page *1951 Ferrari 212 Export Berlinetta Le Mans, by Touring, Chas. No 0112E*

Above *1947 Ferrari 125 replica by Ferrari and on display in the reception at Maranello*

Right *1948 Ferrari 166 Spyder Corsa, this car was campaigned by Prince Troubetskoy and also by Dudley Folland*

Left *1950 Ferrari 166 MM Barchetta, V12 2 liter by Touring, Chas. No 040M*

Below
top *1947 Ferrari Type 166 Inter and* ***bottom*** *engine detail*

Colombo, the same genius responsible for what became the all-conquering Alfa 158 "Alfetta" racer before the war, originally as a project for Ferrari himself. He had rejoined Enzo in 1946, alongside another colleague from the Alfa and Scuderia Ferrari days, Luigi Bazzi, who was now chief engineer. And alongside both of them was another engineer, Aurelio Lampredi.

The 125 wasn't planned as just one model, it was planned as a family of cars, all based on Colombo's superb new V12. That was designed with performance in mind, with a single overhead camshaft for each cylinder bank, racing-style switchback valve springs and a short stroke to encourage high revs. That allowed very nearly 120bhp in racing trim, or almost twice that when supercharged. But Ferrari being Ferrari, the 125 "family" turned out to be a small one—in fact, just two open two-seaters, which would eventually see service in everything from sportscar races to international Grands Prix. One, labeled *Competizione*, had a cycle-fender body (and for Grand Prix-type races could run with no wings at all); the other, labeled *Sport*, had a sleeker, fully enclosed shape by Touring of Milan. Both went racing, and within months the Ferraris started winning.

That story is told later, but the 125s were the start of Ferrari's life as an auto builder proper. The reason Enzo built only two 125s was simple: starting as he meant to go on, he was only really interested in what came next—which, inevitably, meant more power, more performance. By the end of 1947 the 125's V12 had grown to 1.9 liters, giving the new type number 159, but only another two machines were built. Then, in early 1948, the little V12's capacity was pushed up again, to virtually 2 liters, giving birth to the 166—the first Ferrari destined to become a real "production" model.

The first 166, though, was another racing machine, a Spyder Corsa, built in 1948. It was still only the fifth Ferrari built (or, if you reckoned that one of the two 159s was really only a 125 with a bigger engine, only the fourth complete car built), but it was the first ever sold to a customer. And it was a gem. Soon after its launch, the 166 was described as "the most advanced unsupercharged sportscar in the world today." The Spyder Corsa paved the way for other versions, and with its cycle-wings and tacked-on headlights it was equally at home as a sportscar, a racing sportscar, or in stripped single-seater form as a 150bhp Formula Two racer. Its stablemate was a milder "touring" version, the 166 Sport. That had "only" 90bhp, and in typical

***Top** 1950 Ferrari 195S, Chas. No 0060—the only example*

***Above** 1949 Ferrari 195 Inter by Touring*

Ferrari style was sold as a customer model mainly to pay for the racing models, which were all that really mattered to him.

In fact, Enzo originally only sold cars when he needed to pay either his racing expenses or the factory wages, which might account for why he built only two 166 Sports (one spyder, one coupé) before launching the versions of the 166 which made him worthy of the label "manufacturer." Unveiled at the Turin Show in November 1948, the first show Ferrari ever exhibited at, the 166 MM and 166 Inter were another pair of racing and road variations, but this time they were pretty enough, and practical enough, to have a wider appeal. Between 1948 and 1951 he would sell some 38 Inters, plus around 46 examples of the 166 MM in various body styles by various coachbuilders. These would put a useful amount of money into his racing coffers, and the two 166 models demonstrated well how Enzo managed to juggle his racing and selling.

The MM was really a customer racer, named after the classic Mille Miglia road race which Clement Biondetti had won in 1948 with the earlier 166 Sport. The Mille Miglia winner actually had a two-seater coupé body; the production MM had an open two-seater "barchetta" body (literally "little boat") by Touring of Milan, and was in effect a racing machine that could be used on the road. And although any 166 MM, outright racers included, could be used as a road vehicle at a pinch, Ferrari offered both competition and touring versions—the touring with just a bit more trim in the stark cockpit.

The other 166, the Inter, was a coupé, like the Mille Miglia winner in body style but very different in detail. It wasn't the first of the series to use the name, but this 166 Inter became the first to be produced in any real numbers. Normally, Ferrari supplied the chassis and let the customer worry about bodywork, so as time went on there were body variations by several coachbuilders. But like the MM, the Turin Show model was bodied by Touring, and was a road model that could go racing, as a fair few did.

The typical 166 Inter had around 110bhp, the MM about 150. Both had tubular frames, five-speed transmission, wire wheels, solid rear axles on trailing arms and cart springs, and independent front suspension with wishbones and a transverse leaf spring. The brakes were all drums. The Inter, with its longer wheelbase, heavier, more comfortably trimmed body and less powerful engine, was capable of around 105mph. A good 166 MM would nudge 140mph—enough to take the racing version to Ferrari's first Le Mans win, in 1949, while the only slightly slower "production" 166 MMs had supercar performance for a road-usable automobile in the early 1950s.

Model evolution

With this blizzard of early success, Ferrari not only became a major force in international motor racing, he also established himself (whether he enjoyed it or not) as one of the world's most famous makers of exotic production sportscars, and as the 1950s went on, so did the steady evolution of Ferrari's designs.

As early as 1950 he had squeezed 2.3 liters out of the Colombo V12 to create the 195 series. In turn, more power meant more customers, and more customers meant an ever wider variety of models. The open Barchettas, with little or no trim, were usually the racers' choice, while the Inter coupés were aimed more at the wealthy roadgoing market—although, as with all the early Ferraris, there was a good deal of crossover in the way they were used.

Naturally, the 2.3-liter 195 arrived first as a racing model, the 195 Sport in 1950, but the main customer model followed the established name as the 195 Inter. The milder, more luxurious roadgoing Inter coupé, usually with a longer wheelbase than the Sport, was introduced in January 1951 at the Brussels Show. Of all the Ferraris built up to that time, the 195 Inter (again bodied by several styling houses) was arguably the most distanced from its racing cousins. And the biggest change was under the hood.

This was to become yet another familiar pattern. Enzo Ferrari, a stubborn man throughout his life, clung to one philosophy above all others, one rooted in racing: the most important element in terms of making an automobile go quickly is the engine. In his autobiography he wrote, "I have always given great importance to the engine and much less to the chassis,

Left *1951 Ferrari 212 Export Berlinetta Le Mans, by Touring, Chas. No 0112E and* ***above*** *engine detail—this particular car actually has a 225 specification engine*

endeavoring to squeeze out as much power as possible in the conviction that it is engine power which is not fifty percent but eighty percent responsible for success on the track . . . when one has this extra power, chassis deficiencies are not a handicap . . ."

Over the years, that meant Ferrari's racing cars were often the last to adopt new technologies like disk brakes, unibody chassis and, most reluctantly of all, mid engines. In his road cars, too, Ferrari was always conservative with his chassis, sometimes nothing short of pig-headed. But to be fair, Ferrari did make exceptionally good engines, and many of them from the same beginnings.

The man who laid the foundations, designer Colombo, had been pushed out in 1950, just one of many engineers to fall out with the notoriously difficult Enzo over the years. But his classic V12 was still growing, and successive versions would remain at the heart of Ferrari's production range right into the mid-1960s. In 1951, in the 195 Inter, roadgoing power was up to 135bhp and maximum speed to around 115mph—with a bit more on offer with triple Weber carburetors instead of the standard single version. The chassis hadn't changed much, of course, and leaf springs and drum brakes were still the 195 norm, but the Inter had moved on in other ways and become a lot better trimmed, a lot more comfortably equipped, and featured a few more touches of flamboyant styling.

The 195 Inter wasn't around for long, though: only around two dozen cars spanning barely a year. It wasn't that there was anything wrong with it, it was just that now familiar Ferrari theme: onward and upward. Even when the 195 was introduced, in Brussels in 1951, there were other cars alongside it. One was the 340 America, which, as we'll see in Chapter 4, was the start of another direction entirely for the still young Ferrari company. The other was yet another development of the Colombo-engined line, the first since Colombo himself had been dismissed, labeled the 212.

There was a customer competition version, or at least a dual-purpose road/race model, known as the 212 Export, and like the 195 Sport before it, it had a fine racing career. But now the road models were becoming ever more successful too, and naturally that meant another Inter. The 212 took the V12's capacity up to 2563cc, more than a liter bigger than the first 125 version, and for the roadgoing 212 Inter power was up to 150bhp in the early single-carburetor versions, and to 170bhp by 1952 when it took on the triple carburetors and different cylinder heads originally used on the 212 Exports.

***Right** 1951 Ferrari 212 Export Vignale Berlinetta, Chas. No 0111S*

Left *1952 Ferrari 225 Sport Spyder*

In either form, the 212 Inter would top 125mph. That made it one of the world's fastest production vehicles. With Ferrari's growing racing reputation, it gave the still young marque a real mystique, already ranking Ferrari alongside far longer established classic names like Alfa Romeo and Maserati and obliging Enzo Ferrari, however reluctantly, to satisfy a growing demand from wealthy enthusiasts. Production climbed in tandem with capacity. From 1951 to 1952 Ferrari built around 84 212 Inters and another 25 or so 212 Exports, making this by far the biggest series he'd built so far.

Another thing that changed principally to satisfy the road car buyer was the side the steering wheel was on. In his early cars, when racing was the main consideration, and because most circuits run clockwise, Ferrari usually put the steering wheel on the right-hand side. With the 212 Inter it moved to the left, which was better for most markets including the USA. The variety was expanding too, as more customers chose different styles from different styling houses. The first to clothe a 212 Inter was Vignale, but the most important, bodying a roadgoing Ferrari for the first time, was a newcomer: Pinin Farina, who did their first 212 Inter in 1952, went on to do around 20 in all, and within a year would be making bodies for virtually all Ferrari's cars.

Then, hot on the heels of the 212, via the short-lived 225S competition models, another new family arrived which would finally transform Ferrari from small-time constructor to giant in the field. It was the next logical step in the progression, and it became one of the most famous and most successful of all Ferrari families. The first Ferrari 250 was about to burst on to the world stage.

The 250 Family

For Ferrari, 250 turned out to be a very lucky number. It was the next in the progression that had been ongoing from the day Enzo Ferrari built his first car, but where every number so far had been short-lived, this one would run for a remarkably long time. It would finally confirm Ferrari as a big player, and establish the marque as a long-term survivor in the world of exotic sportscars.

In 1947 Ferrari had burst on to the scene with his 1.5-liter 125s. By 1950, the type number had evolved through the "interim" 1.9-liter 159 of late 1947 and the 2-liter 166 of 1948 to the 2.4-liter 195s—all of them descendants of the original 1.5-liter two-camshaft V12 designed by Gioacchino Colombo, and usually referred to as the Colombo engine. Up to the 166 they had gained capacity by increases in both the cylinder bore and the piston stroke. With the 166, the stroke became fixed at 2.315 inches. After that, the capacity was raised simply by increasing the bore size. And Ferrari was able to do that fairly easily, because from the earliest design stage Colombo had built in a lot of scope for growth thanks to very generous spacing between the cylinder bores in his "short" V12 block.

Ferrari didn't keep changing just for the sake of change. It was a bonus to be able to offer road car customers more and more, but, unsurprisingly, the real driving force for change at Maranello was motor sport. Virtually every development made its debut in competition rather than in the showroom. The 1.5-liter 125s, for instance, had been usable for several of the formulas in force when they were launched: they could race without supercharging in 1.5-liter sportscar races, or supercharged in Grand Prix events. So, although Ferrari soon shifted his favors from the blown 1.5-liter to an unblown 4.5-liter engine in the Type 375 Grand Prix car, the 125 had served its purpose of getting Ferrari into business. Then the rules changed to create a Formula Two category for unsupercharged cars of up to two liters, and Ferrari responded first with the 1.9-liter 159, then the full 2-liter 166. From there the 195 and 212 had been natural progressions, through 2.3 to 2.6 liters, with more power for both racing and sportscar customers. But on reaching 250, Ferrari had come to the most effective number so far.

Previous page *Rear of 1960 Ferrari 250 SWB, Chas. No 1993. This car was the first Ferrari imported into Britain by Maranello Concessionaires*

Below
top *Porsche Speedster 356*
middle *1954–57 Mercedes Benz 300SL*
bottom *Jaguar XK-SS*

Increasing production

Employing the usual numbering system (of the capacity of a single cylinder), 250 took Ferrari to the milestone of three liters, or exactly double the point at which the Colombo V12 had started its life. With the stroke still fixed at 2.315 inches and bore now up to 2.894 inches, this was as far as the original Colombo engine would go, but there was certainly no suggestion of this being a stretch too far. This was definitely one of Ferrari's all-time greats.

It was a capacity which fitted any number of bills, and would do so for years to come. Its combination of short stroke and big piston area made it free-revving and powerful, yet still virtually as light and compact as it had been at half the capacity. And it was hugely versatile. By doing little more than changing the camshafts, the carburation and tuning, the 3-liter V12 could be equally at home as everything from a sporting tourer to a World Championship sportscar racer. In motor sport, 250s of one kind or another would win everything worth winning, including Le Mans. On the road, the 250 family would go through more than a dozen major variations and remain at the heart of Ferrari's range for more than a decade. It would also transform the number of cars Ferrari would build.

Above *1953 Ferrari 250 MM, Chas. No 0340*

Before the 250s were born that number hadn't really been high at all, certainly nowhere near as many as Ferrari's already towering reputation might have suggested at the time. In 1949, reporting Ferrari's first Le Mans win, *Autocar* wrote of "production . . . numbered in tens rather than hundreds." The fact was that Ferrari was still only selling what he could be bothered to sell, or what he needed to sell to pay the racing and factory bills. Up to a point, their rarity may have given his road cars an appeal beyond their performance potential for a certain type of buyer, but even Ferrari had to compete for sales in a market which, at the very top of the price ladder, could pick and choose. By the early 1950s the supercar choice (with racing pedigree) included models by the likes of Alfa Romeo, Maserati, Jaguar, Aston Martin, Lancia, Mercedes and Porsche. Compared to Ferrari, even relative newcomer Porsche was already a giant in terms of numbers of cars made and sold.

A couple of years later, in 1951—by which time Ferrari had won their first Grand Prix world titles—*Autocar* wrote about Ferrari production again: "Exploits in Grand Prix and sports car racing have won world fame for Ferrari cars in a very short time; but very few people can speak with first-hand knowledge of their capabilities. Being individually made, they are very expensive, and the total number of cars built so far is probably under three hundred." The true figures, when they emerged years later, show that *Autocar* were overestimating by quite some margin. By the end of 1951 Ferrari's total output was actually less than one-third of the magazine's guess, still well short of 100 cars.

Autocar were a lot nearer the mark when they went on to describe what kind of organization these sales had to support. Ferrari, they said, could boast a large, modern, well-equipped factory with a labor force which, because the cars were both complex and hand-built, was both large and more than usually skilled. In 1951 it took around two weeks to build and test each engine, and some 2,500 man hours to build a "production" car. Even the quality control section had around thirty inspectors and managers, and the racing department—where a single car could take up to 4,000 hours to build, and where expensive development never stood still—employed around forty even more skilled and qualified specialists.

As a result, in commercial terms in those early years, Ferrari was flying very close to the wind indeed. But when the 250 family came along, everything changed. Over the next decade, Ferrari's total output would climb from that early reality of fewer than 100 cars in five years to more than 3,500. And although there were other types too, the majority of them would be 250s of one kind or another.

Below *Interior and engine detail, 1953 Ferrari 250 MM*

Early success

The first of them all, inevitably, was a racer—the 250S racing sportscar. It first appeared in public early in 1952, soon after the previous link in the chain, the 2.7-liter 225S. That car hadn't been around for long, but it had been very successful in competition and had had a production run of around twenty, with Barchetta, Spyder and Berlinetta (literally "small sedan") bodies from Vignale or Touring. The 225 engine had added some new features to Colombo's original design, such as improved valve gear and separate intake ports from the series of larger-capacity V12s designed by Aurelio Lampredi. The one-off 250S which started the 250 ball rolling was actually a Vignale-bodied 225S Berlinetta coupé with the final engine stretch.

On the racetrack, and especially in road races, it was a major success, even by Ferrari's standards. Most spectacular of all was its victory in the 1952 Mille Miglia. The thousand-mile road race around Italy was universally known as one of the toughest events in motor racing, and the 1952 race was one of the most competitive ever, with the mighty Mercedes team back in racing for the first season since the war with the legendary 300SL. The works Mercedes driven by Karl Kling finished second, beaten by a heroic drive from Giovanni Bracco in the Ferrari.

That was all Ferrari needed to launch the 250 into production as the 250 MM, for Mille Miglia, celebrating and capitalizing on Bracco's win. The customer car was unveiled at the Paris Show in October 1952, and although it had more or less the same dimensions and the same chassis layout as the 250S racer, it also carried features that showed Ferrari was taking a bit more notice of what made a car usable on the road. The MM's 3-liter engine with its three Weber carburetors gave a very healthy 240bhp, even in reasonably docile roadgoing tune. Where the

Above and left *1953 Ferrari 250 MM*

250S racer (like most of its predecessors) had a five-speed "crash"-type transmission with no user-friendly synchromesh, the 250 MM had only four speeds, but it did have synchro, making it a lot lighter and easier to use for the "ordinary" driver.

The 250 MM was a genuine supercar by 1952 standards, with a maximum speed of around 155mph and race-bred handling and brakes—although still, of course, from a tubular chassis, leaf springs and drums all round. Ferrari still thought engines were more important than anything else and didn't see any point in changing yet. About half of the three dozen or so 250 MMs built during 1952 and 1953 were Pinin Farina-bodied Berlinettas: all but one of the rest were Vignale-bodied Spyders, the odd one out being another coupé, apparently also built by Vignale. Within a couple of seasons the MMs had become the car to be seen in on the racetrack for the private sports racer, and the 250 was becoming the car to be seen in on the way to the racetrack for the private road car driver.

The first 250 GTs

At the Paris Show in October 1953, Ferrari introduced another car with the type number 250, the 250 Europa, but that was a 250 of a very different kind from the series started with the 250 MM. Instead of the 3-liter version of the classic Colombo V12, it used a smaller version of the Lampredi V12, as described in Chapter 4. But back in the "real" 250 series, in 1954 Ferrari followed the 250 MM with an even more practical roadgoing supercar—what was originally referred to simply as the second series 250 Europa, but what soon came to be known more properly as the 250 GT Europa. And the Colombo-engined 250 GT Europa, as distinct from the Lampredi-engined 250 Europa, was perhaps the most significant of all the early 250s in pointing the way to the kind of car that followed.

It wasn't so much that the mechanical side had changed, more that the character had again shifted slightly, and instead of every example being more or less a one-off, Ferrari was finally starting to make cars in what other people would think of as a proper series. Nevertheless, the 250 GT Europa—introduced in 1954, as was now becoming a Ferrari tradition, at the Paris Show—was still a short run, at only about another 36 examples, into 1955. This time all but one of them (a special coupé built for a member of the Belgian royal family by Vignale) had very similar but not identical coupé bodywork by Ferrari's new partner Pinin Farina. Nine of the Pinin Farina cars were still slightly different, however.

The Pinin Farina-bodied 250 GT Europa was very different under the skin, and because the 3-liter Colombo engine was so much shorter than the 3-liter Lampredi, it could sit on a shorter wheelbase while still having more room inside. Otherwise it looked almost identical to the 250 Europa—which came, of course, from the same styling house. The "egg-crate" grille was becoming a strong identifying feature, and the beautifully proportioned GT coupé looked every inch the 1950s supercar with its long, low hood, low, fastback roofline with wraparound rear window, softly rounded curves and almost total lack of unnecessary decoration.

The GT was a much better car than the "first series" thanks to more power in a smaller, lighter package. This model, again with three Weber carburetors, was good for 220bhp and a maximum speed of 130mph, which may have been some way adrift of the 250 MM but was a huge amount of performance for a car with the new Europa's additional practicality, refinement and proven reliability. Like the 250 MM, it had four speeds and synchromesh, and like all that had gone before it had a tubular chassis, leaf spring rear suspension, and drum brakes. The big change was that the front now used coil springs instead of the old-fashioned transverse leaf, and at the back the chassis ran over, rather than under, the live axle. With the short wheelbase that also made the 250 GT Europa a far more agile and better handling car than the 250 Europa, yet at the same time a car with enough comfort and refinement in the beautifully trimmed, fully road-equipped cabin to be anything from willing long-distance fast tourer to occasional sportscar racer.

***Above and left** 1953 Ferrari 250 Europa by Pinin Farina, Chas. No 0333 EU and **below** engine detail, showing the Lampredi designed V12 of 2963cc*

Out of the trend-setting 250 GT Europa came the next recognizably distinct series, with a twist of its own. It was another 250 GT, introduced at the Paris Show in 1956. Mechanically it was very similar to the Europa, but depending on when it was made it would be called either a Boano or an Ellena model.

Boano and Ellena were coachbuilders who came into the picture because Pinin Farina, by this time Ferrari's more or less dedicated body builder, were becoming victims of their own success. By 1955 they had already styled the 250 GT Europa's successor, which was a refinement rather than a radical redesign. Now, following the system they had already started, the theory was that Ferrari would build the chassis and Pinin Farina would add the more or less standardized coachwork. The catch, temporarily, was that to keep up with demand Pinin Farina needed to build larger production facilities, and until that was done they didn't have the space to work on the 250 GTs. So they farmed the work out.

At first they gave the job to Carrozzeria Boano, a company run by former Pinin Farina employee Mario Boano. But after building some 80 "Boano" 250 GTs, Mario left the company to become boss of Fiat's styling department. From then until the end of the line (in 1958) the remaining fifty or so cars were slightly different in detail and were known as Ellena models after Boano's son-in-law Ezio Ellena, who had taken over the Carrozzeria. By 1958, Pinin Farina's new factory at Grugliasco was completed, and production of the 250 GT Coupé was brought back "in-house" with a new version of what was now the core 250 model. The styling was slightly different, the mechanical layout virtually identical, but production was greatly stepped up, and from late 1958 to the end of the line in 1960, around 350 of the Pinin Farina coupés were built.

Now the 250 family was really on a roll and gathering momentum, and something completely different was waiting in the wings.

Enter the cabriolet

In fact, it took Ferrari a long time to make the next expansion to the growing 250 family, and the fact that it did take so long suggests that even while the early 250s were helping his business to grow so dramatically, the man himself was still less than totally interested in commercial complications. But he was no fool.

The new car, launched in its first guise in July 1957, was the 250 GT Cabriolet. It was Ferrari's first series-built convertible, as opposed to the handful of convertible versions of the early Inters and Exports or the many variations of the more spartan Spyders and Barchettas that had always been part of the range. Those, whatever the label or the model, had more often than not been intended for at least a part-time competition role, so creature comforts were not a big priority. The first production cabriolet, though, was a totally different proposition, combining performance with considerable luxury and, for the first time in a Ferrari, the versatility of a proper, fully-trimmed, fully-weatherproof folding soft top. It had absolutely no pretensions to being a racing car. This was strictly a high-class, high-performance tourer aimed at a very upmarket customer, and with the potential to take Ferrari's sales to another level.

Ferrari hadn't exactly rushed into the soft-top world. In fact, he had had very little to do with the one-off 1953 original save for supplying the chassis. Pinin Farina had put the cabriolet body on it, and it became known as the Ariowitch Cabriolet after the man who commissioned it, but being based on one of the Lampredi-engined 250 Europas rather than on a Colombo-engined 250 GT Europa, the 1953 Ariowitch was no more a "real" 250 GT Cabriolet than the 250 Europa was a real 250 GT Europa. And it obviously hadn't made much of an impression on Enzo, because over the next couple of years not one of the first series of 250 GTs was bodied as a proper cabriolet—although, to be fair, there's no particular evidence either that the market was clamoring for one.

No more came either, directly at least, of the first cabriolet built around a real 250 GT—a car designed and built by Boano for the 1956 Geneva Motor Show but destined to remain strictly another one-off. Then, a year later, came another Geneva Show car, this time by Pinin Farina. With even more flashy and stylized looks than the heavily-finned Boano car it obviously wasn't intended as a production model, and again, just the one was built. This one, though, did have a fairly high-profile life as a road car. It had a long nose with vertical bumper bars flanking a large grille with built-in driving lights, and the tail had a massive horizontal bumper. Like the 1956

Above c.1960 Ferrari 250 Cabriolet, series 2 by Pininfarina, Chas. No 2327GT

Boano show car, its lights were set into the tops of the wings, but its most distinctive styling feature was that the driver's door was cut down, vintage style, supposedly to make room for the driver's elbow.

The most frequent driver, as it turned out, was a famous one: Ferrari's Grand Prix star Peter Collins, who used the sporty Pinin Farina "Spyder" quite regularly. He had two changes made: he swapped the Italian red paintwork for British Racing Green, and he changed the 250 GT's usual drum brakes for a set of the new Dunlop disks. That made this the first Ferrari ever to use disk brakes, and although he was as stubborn as ever about accepting new technology, Enzo Ferrari took notice. The story is that he eventually took the brakes from the Collins cabriolet to try out on a racing Testa Rossa, and having discovered that they actually worked—as sportscar racing rival Jaguar, in particular, had already known for some time—he grudgingly adopted them for both production and racing.

Still, it wasn't quite time for the initial production cabriolet; before that came a few more flights of fancy from Pinin Farina. The first was an even more extreme show car, unveiled early in 1957 and dubbed Spyder Competizione. This one had a small wraparound windshield, a metal tonneau cover over the passenger seat, and a faired headrest behind the driver. Pinin Farina then did two more one-offs, each a bit less flashy than the last, before moving on to the first series of genuine production cabriolets, a run of some 36 cars built between July 1957 and July 1959.

These, finally, were the real thing. Like most 250s they were virtually identical in mechanical make-up and bodywork. From the start they were lovely to look at, and they grew more lovely. In 1958 the front bumpers were simplified and the headlights changed, while in Paris in 1959 the real "second series" arrived with most of the character of the originals but based now on the latest 250 GT coupé, by Pininfarina (as Pinin Farina styled itself from 1958). That also brought an updated version of the classic 3-liter V12, with new valve gear and improved cylinder heads.

Above and right *1959 Ferrari 250 long wheelbase California Spyder, Chas. No 1411 GT*

There was also a new four-speed-plus-overdrive transmission, and disk brakes, although the cabriolet still had old-fashioned lever dampers rather than telescopics.

These were the most luxurious, the most refined and the most expensive 250 GTs yet made. With roomy, comfortable, beautifully trimmed and fully equipped interiors, good soundproofing and reasonable luggage space, they were totally practical long-distance tourers. Eventually, Ferrari even offered a detachable hard top. With 240bhp, they had big performance for a luxury soft top, even though they were arguably further distanced from racing than any car Ferrari had built to date. And commercially they were the biggest sellers so far, adding around two hundred cars to the previous 250 GT Cabriolet output before production ended in 1962.

Which makes it slightly surprising that when the cabriolet did go out of production, Ferrari didn't immediately offer a replacement. That wouldn't arrive for almost exactly two years.

The American market

In the meantime, other cars were taking the 250 from strength to strength. Among them, from 1958 to 1963, there was another convertible, but one quite different in character from the luxurious cabriolet. It was the 250 GT California Spyder, and the clue to why it was so different is there in the name: this was a 250 for America, and America, as ever, wanted something out of the ordinary. With the California Spyder, Ferrari gave them just what they wanted.

America already loved Ferraris: the first had found their way there in the late 1940s. Mainly thanks to sportscars, by the mid-1950s Ferrari's racing reputation was as strong in America as it was in Europe. The road cars were also a big success, both with real enthusiasts and with America's super rich—who might not have been so obsessed with performance but certainly knew all about image. The California Spyder combined big helpings of both, and Ferrari had created it more or less to order for a man who knew what he wanted.

In these early days, two men helped shape Ferrari's market in America: main importer Luigi Chinetti and west coast distributor John von Neumann. Chinetti was a major contributor to Ferrari's racing program; von Neumann was the one who dreamed of what became the California Spyder. He could sell 250 GT Cabriolets, but some of his customers wanted a soft top for the road that they could also use occasionally for racing, which was what mainly attracted many of them to Ferrari in the first place. So von Neumann proposed a car that was more a convertible version of one of the more potent Berlinettas than a topless version of the comfort-biased cabriolet with its less powerful, less sporty coupé underpinnings. Ferrari, only too well aware of the potential market, was happy to co-operate.

By December 1957 he had a prototype, styled by Pinin Farina and at first glance not unlike the cabriolet, but actually very different indeed. The styling was slightly more aggressive, with a more steeply raked windshield, a smaller grille, no bumpers, a functional hood scoop and big air ducts in the front flanks. And under the skin it was different again, based not on the Europa but on the more extreme 250 GT Tour de France Berlinetta, a Ferrari in the old mold which could be used for racing as well as on the road.

The original California Spyder had about 250bhp, and with simpler trim and a few aluminum panels in place of the cabriolet's all-steel shell it was a shade lighter, but not quite as light as the Berlinetta because losing the top demanded additional stiffening. It was quick enough to go sportscar racing American style yet still be reasonably civilized as a road car, and you could wring a bit more performance out with an all-aluminum body and a more highly-tuned version of the V12, both of which you could have off the shelf.

But there was an even quicker California to come, and it arrived in May 1960, after some 46 of the first type had been built. It had the latest V12 with at least 280bhp, and a significantly more effective chassis with a shorter wheelbase, telescopic shocks, disk brakes and overdrive for the four-speed transmission. It was stunningly beautiful and spectacularly quick, with a top speed of 145mph even in road trim. As a production car, until production ended in February 1963, it took total California Spyder numbers past the 100 mark. As a racing car, the short wheelbase model was quick enough to make the Sportscar Club of America move it out of the GT category into the modified sportscar classes.

Below *Ferrari 250 short wheelbase California Spyder, both beautiful and very fast*

The Tour de France and the SWB

Meanwhile, if you wanted a Ferrari that could go racing or be happy on the road but you also wanted a roof, there was another principally European model: the 250 GT Berlinetta, later known (unofficially at least) as the Tour de France. That was the dual-purpose end of the 250 range from 1956 to 1959, the "Berlinetta" tag Ferrari's way of saying that it was a lighter, more spartan, more sporting car than the better equipped coupés. As with the MM, the "Tour de France" part of the name recognized a competition success—in this case Count Alfonso de Portago's win in the 1956 Tour de France with one of the earlier 250 GTs at a time when GT racing was the most important sportscar category.

The 3-liter Colombo V12 as used in the Tour de France had many new features—as most versions did because, of course, at Ferrari engine development in particular never stood still for long. And it's an indication of how popular the "dual-purpose" GT cars were at this time that production up to 1959 amounted to almost 80 cars.

In 1959 they gave way to an even more famous "all-purpose" classic, the 250 GT SWB, or short wheelbase. But although the SWB was also technically speaking a perfectly usable production road car, it was in reality another step towards the outer limits for the 250 GT as a racing model. It was important to Ferrari because after the dreadful accident at Le Mans in 1955 in which more than 80 spectators had died, the focus in world sportscar racing had shifted towards GTs rather than the more exotic prototype racers. These were cars Ferrari could sell in attractive numbers, and the halo effect would sell less exotic models to non-racing customers. Providing, of course, that the racers were seen to be winning.

The 250 GT SWB was Ferrari's way of making sure that they still could. Its "short wheelbase" was short compared to its forerunner the Tour de France, and the transformation began early in 1959 with a handful of cars with a rounder, lower-fronted body shape which Ferrari hoped would be more aerodynamic. Mechanically very similar to any other 250 GT Berlinetta, these "interim" cars were really meant for racing, and they were partly successful, but Enzo Ferrari knew that he needed more. The 250 GT SWB was the result. Styled by Pininfarina, built by Scaglietti, and retaining most of the look of the "interim" cars but with around 20mm chopped from the wheelbase, it first appeared at the Paris Show in October 1959.

The shorter wheelbase made it lighter, nimbler, more aerodynamic, and quicker. Other aspects enhanced its speed: the chassis was stiffer, Ferrari had finally changed to telescopic

Right *1956 Ferrari 250 GT Berlinetta, Chas. No 0557 GT. This car is the de Portago Tour de France winner*

***Above and left** 1957 Ferrari 250 GT Tour de France, Chas. No 0677. This car was 3rd in 1957 Mille Miglia*

shocks, and the 250 GT SWB even had disk brakes. The 3-liter V12, as ever, had improved in detail, and a road-biased version of the SWB typically had 240bhp while racing versions normally quoted 280, with up to 300bhp in the final "SEFAC hot-rod" versions in 1961.

The uncompromising racer was the most important, of course, but interestingly Ferrari also offered a slightly softer variant, knowing that he had to sell enough "production" cars to satisfy the racing homologation rules, which governed acceptance of series-built models into various

Above 1960 Ferrari 250 SWB

classes of racing. That had a mainly steel body with some aluminum panels where the dedicated competition versions were virtually all aluminum, glass where the racers had plastic, fenders where the racers had none, and interior trim where its sister had little or nothing. It also had a slightly milder state of tune and softer suspension, and in place of the long-distance gas tank it could even have some baggage space. It would still top 155mph, though, and of the 165 SWBs built between 1959 and 1962, around 90 were officially designated as road models. If, strictly speaking, the 250 GT SWB was more racer than roadster, it nonetheless qualifies as the ultimate dual-purpose 250 GT.

The last variants

Two more variants on the 250 theme completed the picture, and again, each of them had an appeal all of its own to spread the Ferrari gospel to an even wider audience. The first was the 250 GT 2+2, otherwise known as the 250 GTE, in production from 1960 to 1963. The other was the stunningly beautiful and exceptionally practical 250 GT Berlinetta Lusso, built in substantial numbers from 1962 to 1964. In their own ways, both were as far from the racing image of the marque as a Ferrari could be and still be a Ferrari, but at the same time neither had sacrificed the fundamentals that made a Ferrari a Ferrari.

The GTE came first, and its alternative designation revealed what was different. Unveiled in June 1960, it was Ferrari's first real four-seater, the first family car in the 250 series. It wasn't the first Ferrari with four seats—though the extra two seats in the handful of four-seaters produced to that time had all been strictly token—and it wasn't exactly a full four-seater sedan, but it was a surprisingly usable 2+2, as the name suggested. It was part of the logical progression of Ferrari's output: first racecars, then racecars that could be used on the road, then road models that could be used for racing, and finally road cars. As Enzo Ferrari had grown up, his customers had grown up too, to the point where somebody who had bought one of the earliest Ferraris in the late 1940s or early 1950s might, by the late 1950s or early 1960s, be settled with a young family. But not so grown up or settled that they didn't want a performance automobile.

In the late 1950s, many of Ferrari's rivals could already cater for those customers; it was a market not to be ignored. In 1959 Ferrari and Pininfarina started work on their answer. It would be based on the usual 250 GT underpinnings, and although it would be practical it would still be sporty, so Ferrari insisted the wheelbase couldn't be any longer than that of the Tour de France. To create interior space they moved the engine forward by several inches in an otherwise ordinary 250 GT chassis, which made the car a bit longer in the front. To create some baggage space they made it a bit longer in the tail, so overall it would be about a foot longer than the two-seater Berlinetta, but still with a real GT shape.

One of the short run of prototypes built in 1959 was used to introduce the new design to the public, and considering that the concept was so distanced from motor sport and that even some of his most extreme competition models had been shown first at motor shows, Ferrari's way of unveiling it was slightly odd. The 250 GT 2+2 was revealed as the course car for the Le Mans 24-hour race in June 1960.

Strange as it seemed, it was an inspired way to launch. The idea had been a well-kept secret and it had quite an impact. First impressions were very favorable, and a good few people who until then had thought they were out of the Ferrari market probably decided there and then that they could get back into it. And it didn't harm potential sales at all when Paul Frère and Olivier Gendebien won Le Mans in a 250 Testa Rossa, heading six Ferraris in the first seven places.

The 250 GT 2+2 reached production that October, and for those who had missed it at Le Mans it made the usual Paris Show appearance. It was a big hit. With 240bhp and a top speed of around 135mph, it had impressive performance for a vehicle which had more than enough space

Above *Interior, 1960 Ferrari 250 SWB*

Left *1962 Ferrari 250 GT 2+2 Chas. No 2801*

for two children in the back, plus a reasonable amount of room for two adults over pretty long journeys. It even had ample luggage space, and it was both comfortable and luxuriously trimmed. The only area where it lost out slightly was the handling; the extra weight, the extra length and the need to move the engine forward had made it a bit less nimble, but that was a small price to pay.

It was a surprising automobile, perhaps, for Ferrari, but even more surprising was its commercial success. Over three series, with only minor interior and exterior changes, it sold around 950 units, and by any standards that was a spectacular achievement in an unlikely direction.

The 250 GT Berlinetta Lusso was also slightly surprising. With quite a low profile in its day, and with an unusually short production life of barely eighteen months, in retrospect it is seen not only as one of the handsomest of Ferraris but also as one of the most significant. And after more than a decade in which the various variants of the 250 were Ferrari's core product, the Lusso was the last of the line.

The production version was virtually identical to the prototype, which had been rushed at the last minute on to Ferrari's 1962 Paris Show stand. It was launched soon after the show, styled by Pininfarina, naturally, and built by Scaglietti. Enzo apparently always thought its looks weren't aggressive enough for his idea of a Ferrari, but over the next couple of years, to 1964, around 350 Lusso customers obviously didn't agree with him. It was a car very much of its time, like the 250 GT 2+2 reflecting the fact that although Ferrari's ambitions were still driven by racing, the days were gone when he could treat road models as no more than an irritating sideline. It also reflected the fact that the days when road and racing designs had meaningful overlap were coming to an end.

Which doesn't mean that the Lusso was a poor relation—far from it. It was designed for a sophisticated market, but not for the 2+2 customer with the complication of a family. Inside, it had a brave blend of racing-style bucket seats plus an unusual dashboard layout, with massive speedometer and tachometer dials centrally placed and an array of five minor instruments in front of the driver. In the back there was padded luggage space rather than any pretence at child or occasional adult seats, but the front seats didn't fold forward to allow easy access. Although neither the seats nor the steering wheel could be adjusted for rake, the pedals could be adjusted for reach, as many a race car's could. Significantly, it followed the lead of the 2+2 in moving the engine forward in the chassis, to the benefit of passenger space even if at the expense of the outer limits of sharp handling. So the Lusso had a lot of the 2+2's comfortable, well-equipped and user-friendly character, but it also had some of the visual image of the more focused competition models of the same generation, especially the 250 GT SWB. As such, it embodied the ultimate link between the race cars and the road versions, but without the compromises that had once been acceptable.

Not that it hadn't picked up directions from the racers. Its tubular chassis had hints of 250 GTO, as did its rear suspension, which now had supplementary coil springs as well as the old leafs. And its Colombo V12 was in effect a milder version of the one in the 250 GT SWB, notably using only three twin-choke downdraft Weber carburetors rather than the competition SWB's six. But "milder" in the Lusso's case still meant a very healthy 250bhp, which was more than enough to keep this lovely automobile in the 150mph league.

So, after more than ten years and around two and a half thousand automobiles, the 250 family had been a resounding success. Soon, 275 would be the number heralding the arrival of a new and very different generation.

This page *1963 Ferrari 250 GT Lusso*

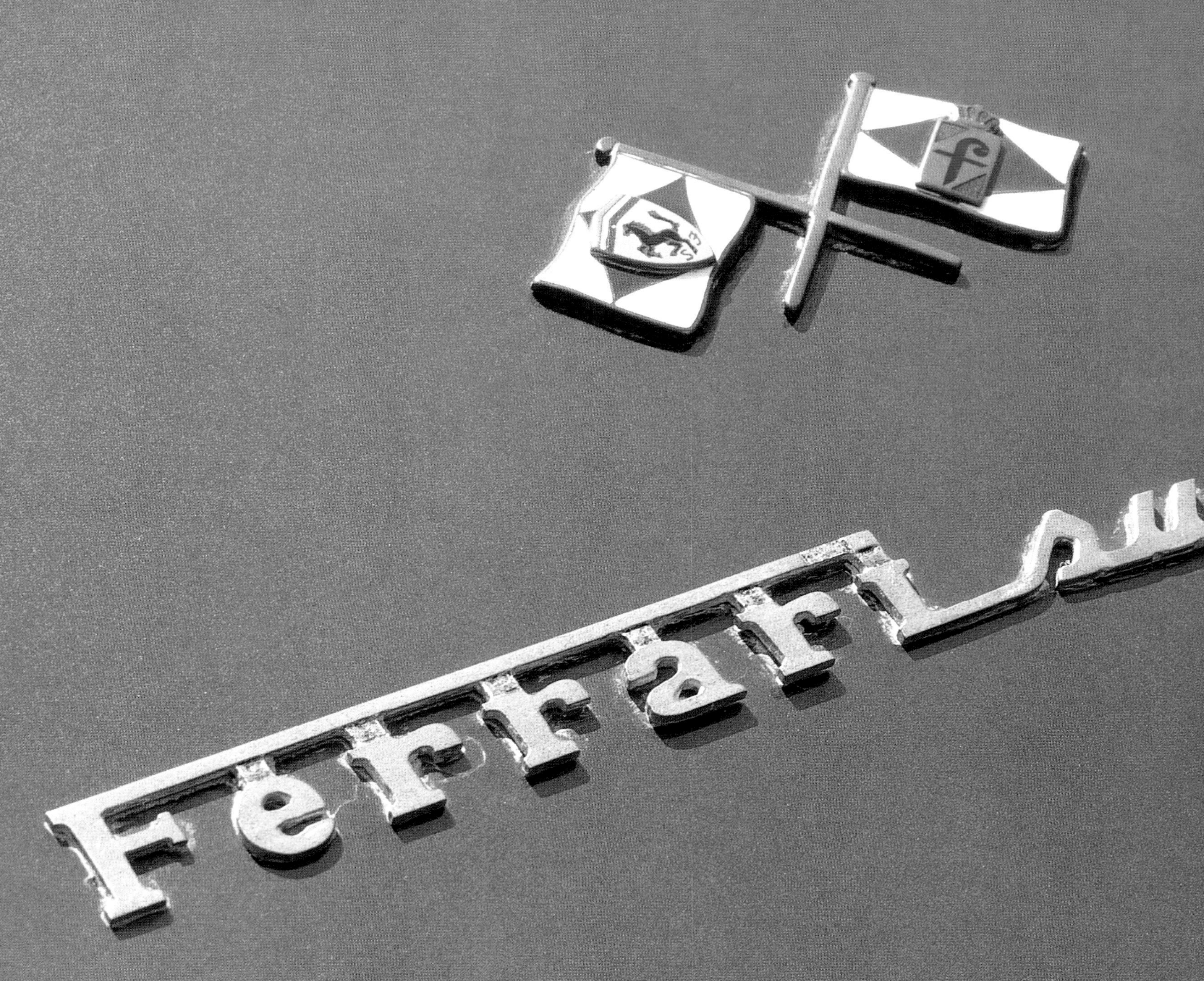
Ferrari

The Big V12s

Enzo Ferrari may have had a huge talent for finding engineering geniuses, but he wasn't always so good at holding on to them. Although the classic V12 designed by Gioacchino Colombo was the basis of many of Ferrari's most successful models for more than a decade, by 1950 Colombo had left the company. Early in his memoirs, Ferrari described him as "my old friend," but in the end they fell out, and Colombo moved on—first to Maserati, and later to what was left of Bugatti, just before that company disappeared.

Enzo was unlikely to have been sentimental about the parting, and unlikely to have lost much sleep over the implications for his future products. After all, he already had the Colombo V12, and with or without its creator that would see Ferrari through the next decade and more. What's more, never being a man to put all his eggs in one basket, virtually from the start Ferrari had another string to his bow. As well as Colombo, he had another star.

Lampredi's impact

Having Aurelio Lampredi allowed Ferrari to develop in two directions at once. Eventually the Colombo engine grew to twice its original 1.5 liters, and as Ferrari himself acknowledged, its basic design would be recognizable in Ferrari V12s far beyond that. On the other hand, the Colombo engine's evolution took time, and Enzo Ferrari, in racing especially, rarely had much of that.

Brilliant as the early Colombo engine was without a supercharger in the early sports racing and road models, in supercharged Grand Prix form it wasn't as good as Ferrari had hoped it would be. It was certainly no match for the vehicle he and Colombo had created before the war for Alfa Romeo. As the 159, that "Alfetta" was uncatchable in Grands Prix. So Ferrari looked at the alternative route, the big unblown engine, and that was Lampredi's speciality.

Lampredi was with Ferrari for around seven years. He had started as Colombo's assistant right at the company's beginnings, and while Colombo designed the first 125 it was Lampredi's team who built it. He left briefly in 1947 but returned less than a year later, by which time Colombo's V12 was well into its stride everywhere except on the Grand Prix trail. Starting from the 1.5-liter Colombo V12, and with unblown power in mind, Lampredi was given the job of creating an engine that could run to considerably larger capacities than would be possible from the very compact Colombo engine with its closely spaced cylinder bores. He designed an engine which was still a 60-degree V12, but which had a much longer block, and so had room for considerably bigger cylinder bores.

Lampredi's engine had many other differences too: in the cylinder heads, in the valve gear, in the oil system, and in the way the cylinder liners were fitted into the cylinder block. It started life at more than twice the capacity of the first Colombo V12, at 3.3 liters, and appeared first in racing, in the 275S at the 1950 Mille Miglia, then with the same capacity in the old 125 F1 chassis for its first Grand Prix outing, in Belgium in June 1950. By the following month, the Grand Prix version was up to 4.1 liters in a new chassis of its own, and by September had reached the full 4.5 liters allowed by the regulations. It became the engine with which Ferrari finally beat the Alfas, when Froilan Gonzalez won the British Grand Prix at Silverstone in 1951. With that victory, Ferrari proved he could beat the best.

But winning brought other pressures, partly in terms of financing the racing, partly from wider recognition of the marque, not least from potentially the biggest market of all, America, which in the early post-war years had a lot more money to spend than Europe.

Previous page *1965 Ferrari 500 Superfast, Chas. No 500SF 6673*

Below *Ferrari 125 F1 1948–50*

Left c.1951 Ferrari 340 America Touring Berlinetta. Photographed at the Ferrari factory, 1990

More power to America

America had taken notice of Ferrari virtually from day one. They might not have known (or cared) much about Grand Prix racing, but after World War Two US troops returning from Europe brought back with them a newfound love of European-style sportscars and sportscar racing. So while the top levels of American motor sport were (and are) still mostly focused on oval racing, European-type circuit racing, usually on disused wartime airfields, became a boom area at club racing level. That was one reason why America took particular notice when Ferrari won the 24-hour Le Mans race for the first time, in 1949, because in the late 1940s Le Mans had a worldwide fame even Grand Prix racing couldn't match.

Sharing the driving in that race were Englishman Lord Selsdon and Italian-born American Luigi Chinetti. Chinetti had already won Le Mans in 1932 and 1934, driving Alfa Romeos when Enzo Ferrari was Alfa's man. Now Chinetti was a major automobile dealer in New York. As soon as he knew that his old friend Ferrari was going to build his own vehicles, he ordered a first batch for what he reckoned would be an enthusiastic American market. The first Ferrari he ever imported, the 166 Spyder Corse, became a race winner when Briggs Cunningham won with it at Watkins Glen in 1949. That was the first of a flood of American successes which, as in Europe, helped establish a market not only for Ferrari's racers, but for his road models too.

America, however, didn't necessarily want the same kind of Ferrari road models as Europe. Outside the really knowledgable racing crowd, America didn't understand small, super-sophisticated engines; America understood size. On racetracks and in showrooms, the popular cry was "there's no substitute for cubic inches." Which is where Lampredi's V12 family comes in. Ferrari had originally seen it as the answer to his racing problems. America saw it as much more its type of thing than the tiny Colombo V12, and Ferrari was happy to give American customers what they wanted.

Below 1954 Ferrari 375 Plus

Above and right 1953 Ferrari 375 MM Spyder, Chas. No 0362AM. This car ex Ibanez/Valiente

At the Paris Show in October 1950 Enzo Ferrari unveiled his first Lampredi-engined road car, the 340 America. It was a Barchetta, with a body by Touring, though the short production run of around 25 vehicles built through 1951 offered a wide range of bodies, including Barchettas and Berlinettas, from Ghia and Vignale as well as Touring. Although some stayed in Europe, most came to America.

The chassis was a suitably bigger and more robust version of what was then standard Ferrari fare: a tubular ladder with independent front suspension, solid axle rear suspension, leaf springs all round, and drum brakes all round. The engine was a 220bhp, 4.1-liter version of Lampredi's V12, driving through five-speed manual transmission. It gave a typical roadgoing version of the 340 America a maximum speed of more than 140mph, and plenty of them had a good deal more power—with a spot of racing in mind.

And quite a few of them went racing. In 1951 Piero Taruffi and Luigi Chinetti took victory in the 1951 Carrera Panamericana, the 2,000-mile Mexican road race, one of the fastest, most gruelling and most dangerous races in the world—and, of course, one of the best known to American enthusiasts. The winner wasn't a 340 America, it was a Colombo-engined 212 Inter, but the win prompted Ferrari to build four race-prepared 340s for the 1952 Carrera, as 340 Mexicos, in honor of the 1951 victory. Although the three Berlinettas and one Spyder, all bodied by Vignale, were strictly speaking built for racing, they were also quite usable on the road. Only one, a Berlinetta, survived the 1952 Carrera, to finish third—appropriately enough shared by Chinetti. On the racing side it was succeeded by an even more powerful development, the 340 MM, which went on to win the Mille Miglia after which it was named, before evolving into the 4.5-liter 375 MM.

On the roadgoing front the original 340 America gave way to a series that was more biased towards comfort, convenience and life on the road: the 342 America. Introduced in 1952, it

Below *1959 Ferrari 410 Superamerica, and interior*

Above 1963 Ferrari 400 Superamerica, Chas. No 4443

wasn't a success. It had a slightly longer, wider chassis, a stronger but less sporty four-speed transmission, and more weight to be dragged around by a less powerful version of the 4.1-liter V12. Only half a dozen were built, five bodied by Pinin Farina, the other by Vignale. If they proved anything, it was that even the greatest Ferrari fans wouldn't buy an overweight, underpowered Ferrari.

No one could make such accusations stick on the next of the Lampredi line. When the 375 America was unveiled in Paris in 1953, capacity was up to 4.5 liters and power output to a full 300bhp—easily the most powerful production Ferrari yet offered, and much more what the customer had in mind. Not many customers, admittedly, because a production run which stuttered on into 1955 saw only a dozen 375 Americas roll out of Pinin Farina, Ghia and Vignale's coachbuilding factories, but the one thing nobody complained about with the 375 was lack of performance.

For the Lampredi line, the only way now was onward and upward. When Ferrari finally replaced the quick-driving but slow-selling 375 he had clearly decided that there was money to be made at the very top end of the market by giving people precisely what they wanted, virtually customer by customer. So the new 410 Superamerica was a different kind of automobile again.

Introduced in January 1956, it was the motoring equivalent of a tailored suit. Over three series, and running through to 1959, only about 40 were built, but while all were hugely expensive and fairly special, almost no two were identical. Performance was not an issue, thanks to at least 340bhp from a 5-liter version of the long-block V12, which offered more than enough excitement for most drivers in a chassis which now had coil springs at the front but still had the old solid axle and cart springs at the back, not to mention the old-fashioned lever-type shock-absorbers. It was a big car, too, on the long wheelbase of the old 375 and usually with bodywork, mostly in the form of Pinin Farina coupés, that wasn't intended to hide the 410's light. The second series started late in 1956 and was mainly distinguished by a shorter wheelbase, while the third series, which started in 1957 and saw the 410 through to the end of production in

1959, had bigger changes: a revised engine with new cylinder heads which took power up to around 360bhp, and bigger brake drums to cope with it all.

Then, within the 410 Superamerica family, there was another new direction, starting with a dramatic show car from 1956.

The Superfast concept

At that year's Paris Show, Pinin Farina rebodied one of the early Superamericas into a stunning concept automobile which they called the Superfast. With five liters and 380bhp under the hood from the racing version of the 410, the 410 Sport, it undoubtedly would have been super fast, and whether it was or not, it certainly looked it. Dramatically finished in off-white with a mid-blue surrounding the vehicle below the bumper line, it was one of the most aggressive-looking road designs Ferrari and Pinin Farina had ever built. The hood went on for ever, the huge grille was flanked by faired-in headlights, the fastback coupé roof was short and low, the hood scoops and side ducts big and prominent. And just like a generation of other American-influenced automobiles in the mid-1950s, its profile was dominated by a pair of towering, sharp-edged tail fins. There wasn't too much doubt as to which market it was aimed at.

But this was only a start. The 1956 Superfast remained a spectacular one-off, and so did each of two further Pinin Farina Superfast concepts which followed. The first appeared at the Turin Show in 1957 as the 4.9 Superfast. Mechanically it was similar to the incredible original, but its styling was toned down slightly with the big tail fins chopped down and a more conventional roofline than the first model, which had had no front pillars and a huge, wraparound windshield. Then, to complete the Superfast styling hattrick, at the 1960 Turin Show Pininfarina (as the styling house had, of course, become known) produced the Superfast II.

Based on the newly introduced 4-liter 400 Superamerica which had taken over from the 410, the Superfast II was another stepping stone to a production Superfast, but strictly speaking it was out of the family line because it actually used a Colombo-type V12 (all the others were Lampredis)—a far bigger Colombo V12 than had so far appeared anywhere else, but a Colombo engine nonetheless. Aside from that major mechanical difference, it also had a slightly different character as it was rather more restrained in styling terms, and with hindsight was the first step towards building a production version of the Superfast. It was followed by two more minor updatings of the theme, the Superfast III and Superfast IV, both of which Pininfarina showed off in 1962. Version III, like version II, had retractable headlights; IV had a totally different four-headlight design which made the long front end look even longer.

Then finally, in 1964, the Superfast name re-emerged as a production reality, now called the 500 Superfast and even more spectacular in some respects than the show models that led the way. Where those had been strictly Pinin Farina (or Pininfarina) only, on "borrowed" Ferrari chassis, this one was the real thing, another classic Ferrari–Pininfarina partnership—Ferrari providing the underpinnings, Pininfarina adding the clothes. It had large doses of 400 Superamerica in its shape, but look more closely and it was quite different, with a chopped-off "Kamm" tail (named after the aerodynamics genius who had invented it) and a more conventional, uncovered headlight layout. Still, although it was quite understated by earlier standards and the big, flashy fins had long since vanished, there was no mistaking that the new Superfast was still aimed at America—if for no other reason than what was under the hood.

Below *1965 Ferrari 500 Superfast, Chas. No 500SF 6673, also showing interior and engine bay*

This was another completely new breed of Ferrari V12, seen nowhere else but in this car. It wasn't exactly a Colombo engine, nor was it exactly a Lampredi engine; rather, it combined the best features of both. It had the Lampredi "long block," similar to that in the 410 Superamerica, but it had Colombo-type cylinder heads. More importantly so far as the non-technical customer was concerned, it was the biggest production engine Ferrari had built (indeed, the biggest they would build for decades to come) and the most powerful by some way, with about as much power as you could buy in a road car in 1964: virtually a full five liters and producing 400bhp. That was fed through a four-speed plus overdrive transmission, which was later upgraded to a true five-speed type. Even in an automobile as large and relatively heavy as the 500, this powertrain gave staggering performance for its day, including a top speed of 160mph with the highest of the optional final-drive ratios. If you settled for a lower top speed, you could have the ultimate in mind-blowing acceleration. Or you could always settle for a balance between the two.

But this wasn't some temperamental, stripped-bare pseudo racer, this was the world's fastest grand tourer, with the emphasis on the grand. Its chassis had the ongoing layout of double wishbones and coil springs at the front, solid axle and leaf springs at the back—although at least they were now controlled by telescopic shockabsorbers. Even more reassuringly, the 500 had disk brakes all round.

It was a big performer that deserved, and performed best on, a big stage. On smaller, tighter roads, it wasn't an easy car to drive. It was big, and until it got into its giant stride its controls were too heavy to be really comfortable. But show it a wide, open, fast road and the 500 Superfast was a different proposition entirely. The massive engine, as well as having massive power, had massive flexibility; as a long-legged mile-eater the 500 was colossal. And it still had a lot of sporty Ferrari character, with plenty of high-speed feel, loads of grip from some of the biggest tires you could find on any road automobile in the early 1960s, impeccably rapid and faithful steering responses, and those very strong brakes.

Left *1965 Ferrari 500 Superfast. This was Peter Sellers' car*

It had one more particularly big number about it: the price, which was around twice as much as that charged for a contemporaneous Rolls-Royce. It was easily the most expensive model in the Ferrari range, and one of the most expensive vehicles in the world—not only among supercars but among automobiles of any kind. To cater for the kind of customer who had that sort of money to spend, the 500 didn't hold back on the creature comforts. The roomy cabin (roomy for two, notionally with room in the back for two small ones) was impeccably trimmed in leather, wood, and wool carpets, and at first glance the interior was almost more limousine than staggeringly fast racer.

Not surprisingly, perhaps, Ferrari didn't sell many of them—only 36 between 1964 and 1966. Having said that, looked at another way, they probably sold more than anyone would have imagined at the start of the run had you simply read them the specification and the price tag. One other thing, too: the list of owners may not have been long, but it was very high profile, from British actor Peter Sellers to the Aga Khan and the Shah of Iran, who had two. Even among Ferraris it was something out of the ordinary, and it was a worthy way to crown the big V12 line.

Which was probably how Ferrari should have left it, except that there was one more flowering of the long-block line to come, the 365 California. In any other circumstances it would probably have been seen as a classic; after the 500 Superfast it was an anticlimax. It was introduced at the Geneva Motor Show early in 1966 and was different from the 500 in just about every facet of its character. For starters, it was a cabriolet, and by Pininfarina standards it was a fussy, unbalanced design with an uncomfortable mixture of curves and angles. Capacity had dropped back to 4.4 liters in what was more a stretched version of the Colombo block than a real Lampredi one, and power was down to "only" 320bhp. It was no lightweight either, because the one thing that had carried over was the luxury feel, and putting back the stiffness lost by chopping off a hard top always adds an awful lot of weight. Moreover, its long wheelbase and increasingly outdated cart-spring rear suspension meant that by Ferrari standards it was a fairly mediocre handler.

When the end came, in 1967, just fourteen had been sold. Fortunately for the Ferrari faithful, by that time the choice was no longer restricted to small or big V12s. Things had moved on again.

GB
URA
426M

The 250 Heritage

Although the stretchability of the original Colombo engine had apparently come to an end with the 250 versions (which, after all, had had the same capacity for more than a decade), the spirit of the first Ferrari family had plenty of life in it yet. Another three generations' worth, in fact. As it turned out, that amazing engine wasn't quite finished even then. Incredibly, before he would finally have to change it, Ferrari again managed to squeeze a few more cubic inches from the classic 250 block. The stroke was the same as it had been for so many years, at 2.315 inches, yet somehow Enzo found another whisker between the cylinders to increase the bore size one more time.

The Lamborghini feud

At the Paris Show (where else?) in 1964, Ferrari finally unveiled the vehicle to succeed the long-running 250 family, and it was a gem. Or, more accurately, it was two gems, because this time Ferrari launched two production versions simultaneously, both elegantly bodied by Pininfarina. One was dubbed 275 GTB, the other 275 GTS. The 275 stood, in Ferrari's usual one-cylinder shorthand, for the new engine capacity —a total of 3.3 liters; GTB stood for Gran Turismo Berlinetta, GTS for Gran Turismo Spyder. And the GTS wasn't just a convertible version of the GTB, its look was actually quite different, more like the earlier cabriolets or 2+2s. It wasn't quite true, either, that the 275 V12 was a total reinvention. These 1964 275s were actually the bridge from 250 to the next capacity stretches.

The 275 was a design to keep Ferrari at the forefront of the exotic automobile business, and hanging on to that position was looking increasingly precarious. By 1964, Ferrari had a new and serious rival looking over his shoulder, a tractor maker turned supercar builder from nearby Sant'Agata Bolognese, one Ferrucio Lamborghini.

According to legend, this was more than a business confrontation, it was personal. Lamborghini, a man twenty-odd years Enzo Ferrari's junior but born barely twenty miles from

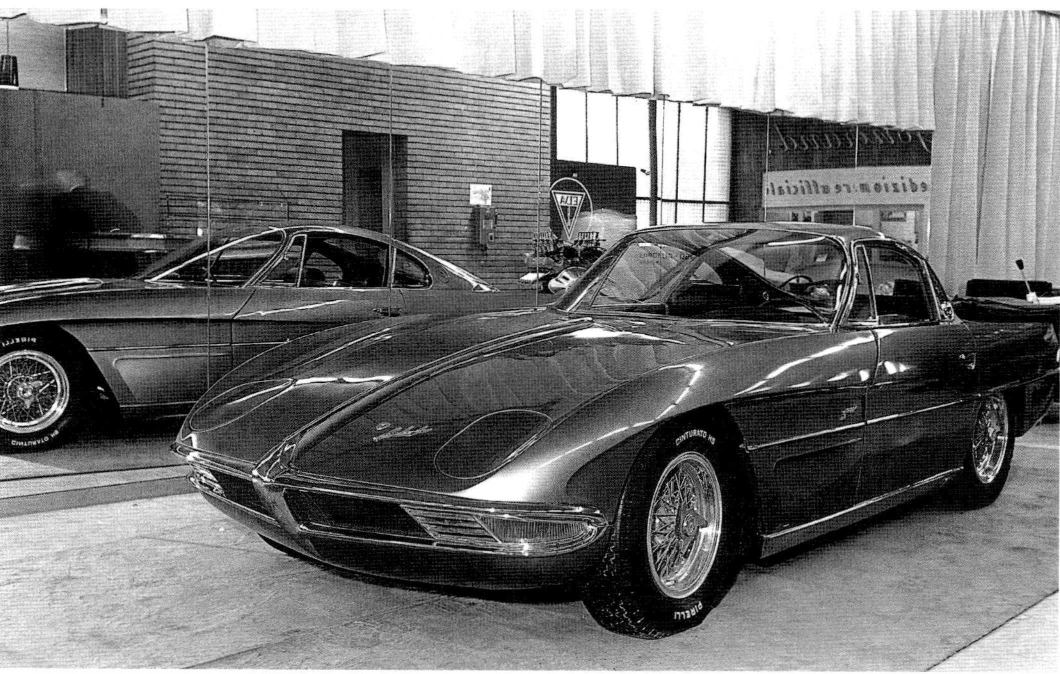

***Previous page** 1973 Ferrari 365 Daytona*

***Right** 1963 Turin Show: the first Lamborghini 350 GTV*

Above 1965 Ferrari 275 GTB SWB Chas. No 7413

Below Lamborghini 400 GT

where Ferrari himself had first come into the world, was, in his way, every bit as powerful and determined a character as his long-established rival. He had started his business soon after the war, building small tractors from surplus military vehicles, just as Ferrari's first employer at the end of the First World War had converted military vehicles into civilian ones. From there, Lamborghini became a leading manufacturer of conventional tractors and branched out into making industrial and domestic heating and air-conditioning equipment. He was successful, respected and rich. And he was a Ferrari owner. In fact, he owned a fair number of exotic vehicles, but it was his Ferraris that prompted him to take his next giant step—or, rather, Ferrari himself.

It is no secret that Enzo Ferrari wasn't the easiest man in the world to deal with, even, perhaps especially, if you were a Ferrari customer. The Old Man, as he had already come to be called, never fully grew out of his original philosophy, that racing was all that really counted and selling to customers was a necessary evil to support it. He didn't have much interest in customers, nor did he have much time for customers who had problems with his automobiles.

Ferrucio Lamborghini had had problems with his Ferraris, and being a man who expected his expensive toys to work, he had informed Ferrari of those problems. Ferrari, it is said, dismissed Lamborghini totally, telling him to stick to tractors and leave the thoroughbreds to somebody who understood them. Lamborghini was less than impressed by such treatment, and went off to hatch his plan. He would beat Ferrari at his own game by building a Lamborghini car.

With most people a bruised ego and a plan would have been as far as it went, but not Lamborghini. He had the passion to build his concept, he had (or could create) the facilities, and he had the money. He began to recruit engineers, Gianpaolo Dallara among them, to create a chassis, and the brilliant Giotto Bizzarini, father of Ferrari's legendary 250 GTO, to turn his dreams into reality. Come the Turin Show in 1963, Lamborghini was able to show his first model, the sensational 350 GTV.

It stopped the exotic automobile world dead in its tracks. From a clean sheet of paper, in a matter of only a few months, Lamborghini's team had created a masterpiece, a stunning GT with

***Top** 1966 Ferrari 275 GTB Longnose and* ***above** interior*

sharp, modern lines by Scaglione and a mechanical specification which must surely have made even Ferrari pause for thought. Dallara had given the first Lamborghini chassis something Ferrari's 250s had never had: all-round independent suspension as part of a state-of-the-art package. And the specification of Bizzarini's stunning new V12 was way ahead of anything Ferrari had so far offered for the road—so much so, in fact, that many people automatically assumed Lamborghini was headed straight for the racetrack too.

That wasn't the case, and, except for a few experiments, it never became the case. Lamborghini wasn't interested in racing, but he was passionately interested in outdoing Ferrari's road vehicles. His new V12 had four camshafts where Ferrari's still only had two, and even though it was purely meant as a production engine, it was bristling with thoroughbred racing design features that would have made Ferrari look twice. It was also bigger than Ferrari's staple 250 V12s, at 3.5 liters, and it was a good deal more powerful, at around 360bhp in its first, show guise, with six downdraught twin-choke Weber carburetors and wild camshafts. Although it was toned down (as was the styling, now by Touring) for the first production versions, known as the 350 GT, it was still more than a match for any mainstream 250 engine. It was also refined and reliable.

The design was in production by 1964 and it was an instant success, especially technically, which was surely what riled Ferrari most. He would never have admitted that the newcomer gave him any concerns, but clearly Ferrari had to respond. So Lamborghini, more than any other factor, was probably the spur for Ferrari to move on.

The 275

At 3.3 liters, 275 capacity still wasn't quite up to Lamborghini's entry-level 3.5, and of course the 275 V12s still had only a single overhead camshaft on each cylinder bank, but it was a brilliant engine nonetheless. With three twin-choke carburetors Ferrari's quoted figure, 280bhp, matched Lamborghini's toned-down production 350 GT. That figure was for the GTB; the slightly more docile GTS offered 260bhp, but that was more in line with its character as a fast

open tourer. Ferrari also offered a six-carburetor version which wasn't so flexible or refined for road use but which had 300bhp and made the 275 something the Lamborghini definitely didn't pretend to be—another automobile with competition potential.

Some 275s certainly did go racing, and the story of those is told in more detail in the later racing chapters, but the vast majority of the 455 GTBs and two hundred or so GTSs built between 1964 and 1966 were intended purely as roadsters. And there was more to them than just the bigger engine. Finally, Ferrari had recognized that the solid-axle rear suspension he had used from day one was bordering on the prehistoric, so at last he gave a road model the kind of all-independent suspension he had been using on the racers for many years (again, he would

Top *1966 Ferrari 275 GTS, Chas. No 07791*

Left *1965 Ferrari 275 GTB* Speciale *Series 1 GTB/C, Chas. No 07517, one of only 10–15 lightweight short front* Competizione Berlinettas, *and* ***below*** *engine detail*

Right *The gorgeous Pininfarina lines of a 1968 Ferrari 275 GTB/4, Chas. No 10835*

undoubtedly have maintained that the fact that Lamborghini had all-independent suspension was just a coincidence).

It was certainly the best Ferrari production chassis so far. There were coil springs, double wishbones and telescopic shock absorbers at each corner, and getting rid of the old-fashioned rear axle allowed Ferrari to make big changes to the engine and transmission layout. The transmission had usually been fixed to the back of the engine, between driver and passenger in the middle of the car; with his new independent rear suspension Ferrari could separate the transmission from the engine and mount it at the back with the final drive, forming a rear "transaxle." Once he had solved early problems with alignment and rigidity, that gave better weight distribution for better handling, and because he could reduce the size of the transmission tunnel it conferred more cabin space. The only downside was that the longer linkage meant the shift was never quite as quick and positive as it had been with the old, direct change.

As an overall package the 275 was stunning, even alongside the show-stopping Lamborghini

350 GT. In either closed or open form the styling was a superb blend of elegance and aggression with absolutely no unnecessary decoration and more than a hint of the competition connection, which was the one thing Lamborghini lacked. It was a magnificent successor to the 250s, combining the character of an outright performer like the 250 GT SWB with the comfort and refinement of designs like the Lusso and the Cabriolet. It was also very, very quick, with a top speed of 150mph—and now with a chassis which could cope with that better than ever. On the other hand, it did show up what was to become a familiar new problem as road vehicles reached speeds that a few years previously were confined to race cars. At speed, the steering of the original short-fronted version of the 275 used to get worryingly light as the front lifted aerodynamically. In 1965, along with other detail body changes, the 275 was given a slightly longer front end to kill this high-speed lift. As 150mph and more became a reality for roadsters, aerodynamics became as important as engines and chassis.

Power and performance were now on another upward spiral. Competition versions of the 275 GTB had extra power and less weight, with more aluminum panels than the normal model, which used aluminum only for doors, hood and trunk, and was otherwise built in steel. In 1966 Ferrari introduced another version meant mainly for GT racing, the 275 GTB/C (for Competizione). It was closely based on the standard GTB, because that was the only way Ferrari, having bent the rules fairly outrageously with some of his 250 racing derivatives, could get the GTB/C past the rule makers. But it was a short-lived and rare model which he dropped within a year, and in 1966 he also dropped the 275 GTS. Things were moving on again.

The 330 branch

Each model had its own replacement, heading in different directions: the competition-bred 275 GTB/C was replaced by the 275 GTB/4, the 275 GTS by its first cousin in another major family, the 330 GTS.

Below *1966 Ferrari 330 GT 2+2, Chas. No 6497, shown here with a 1935 De Havilland Hornet Moth*

The 2+2 Family

The luxurious, spacious "family" Ferraris, which began with the 365 GT/4 2+2 in 1972, may have been less glamorous and less obviously performance-oriented than most Ferraris, but these fine V12-engined "sedan" were still Ferraris through and through.

That 365 GT/4, launched in Paris in 1972 and in production until 1976, wasn't the first 2+2 Ferrari had ever made, but it was a Ferrari 2+2 with a difference. Before this one, in pretty well every previous 2+2 the "+2" part had been largely token, signifying that it could accommodate small children and was just about bearable for a small adult over a shorter distance. People with more than two in the family had always bought 2+2 Ferraris in worthwhile numbers, maybe because driving a 2+2 Ferrari was better than driving no Ferrari at all. What made the 365 GT/4 2+2 different was that all four seats were actually usable, yet the car still had real Ferrari performance, real Ferrari style, and a real Ferrari engineering pedigree.

The 365 GT/4 2+2 took up where the 365 GT 2+2 had left off in 1971, but it was a lot roomier and more practical even than that model. Based on the four-cam 4.4-liter 365 GTC/4, it had a beautifully crisp Pininfarina two-door body on a slightly longer and wider chassis, but in a package that was slightly lower and shorter overall with much smaller front and rear overhangs. It had rear legroom and headroom, and with 320bhp it had real performance, with a 150mph maximum.

It didn't sell in huge numbers – just 525 according to the factory – but it did well enough to carry on, in spirit, into several more generations. The 400 GT which followed it at the Paris Show in 1976 looked virtually identical, and was, except for more space and improved comfort inside, plus a capacity increase to 4.8 liters, lifting power to 340bhp. Far more radically, as an alternative to the usual five-speed manual transmission, Ferrari offered the 400 GT with a three-speed automatic option—the first automatic ever offered in a Ferrari. Strange though it may seem, it suited the character of the 2+2 perfectly well, and whether the purists liked it or not, in this family at least the auto option was there to stay.

In other respects, the series followed a familiar pattern. Towards the end of 1979 the 400i (by that time the last Ferrari with a V12 rather than a flat-12 engine) replaced Weber carburetors with Bosch fuel injection, dropping to 310bhp but with cleaner emissions. At Geneva in 1985 Ferrari introduced the 412, son of 400. Again you had to look hard to spot the changes, but increasing capacity to 4.9 liters had taken power back to its earlier peak, at 340bhp, and the brakes now had ABS as part of the relaxed driving package, which still included the automatic option plus power steering and air-con. But in 1989, after building almost three thousand examples in total of the 2+2 family from 365 to 412, Ferrari finally pulled the plug.

***Top** 1989 Ferrari 412 and **bottom** 400 interior showing automatic transmission. Ferrari never built any 400 series convertibles: this is a conversion which also has non-standard interior trim*

Left *1967 Ferrari 330 GTC, Chas. No 11079*

Below
top *This is an ultra-rare 1966 Ferrari 365 California. Only two right-hand-drive examples were built out of a total of 14 cars*
bottom *1970 Ferrari 365 GT 2+2, Chas. No 12897*

The 275 GTB/4 brought another Ferrari road model first: the "4", standing for four camshafts. It also had racing-style "dry-sump" lubrication and six twin-choke downdraught carburetors, to push power to a full 300bhp, fighting back against Lamborghini. To many people, any 275 was already one of the best handling and least temperamental Ferraris ever built. The GTB/4 lost none of the new chassis's brilliance and added even more performance.

But if the racy, high-revving character of the 275 GTB/4 wasn't for you, there was now an alternative. The 330 line had actually broken cover initially as long ago as the very end of 1963, when Ferrari built around fifty vehicles, all coupés, all bodied by Pininfarina and looking virtually identical to the 250 GTE. This largely forgotten first 330 was labeled the 330 America, possibly because that was where Ferrari expected most of them to go. It introduced a new 4-liter V12, a Colombo engine in layout but with the block lengthened to make space for bigger cylinder bores. Then, in January 1964, the new 4-liter engine was used to transform the 250 GT 2+2 into the far better known 330 GT 2+2, although still with the non-independent rear axle of the 250 series rather than the all-independent set-up of the still-to-be-announced 275s. Originally it had four headlights, like the Superfast IV concept car, but not everyone liked those. During 1965 the Mk II version swapped them for a much neater two-headlight shape, and at around the same time the original four-speed-plus-overdrive transmission was replaced by a five-speed type. Whether they'd liked the early looks or not, people bought the comfortable, quick and usable 330 GT 2+2 to the tune of some 1,100 examples before production ended in 1967.

This, though, was not the classic 330 family. That was subtly different, and even better. While the 250-based 330 GT 2+2 was still being made, Ferrari introduced a different generation of 330s, this time following on from the all-independent 275s. It began with the GTC coupé, unveiled at the Geneva Motor Show in March 1966. Then the GTS Spyder appeared, on a familiar stage: in Paris, in October 1966. Having both GTC and GTS versions in the range again gave Ferrari maximum commercial opportunity, allowing him to sell around another 700 of the 330 series, the majority of them coupés.

This time, too, the two versions, GTB and GTS, were more similar than the 275 twins had been to each other, above as well as below the skin. The GTS hadn't become more sporty, but the GTB had become less of a racer clone than it had been in the 275 family. Not that either of them didn't have performance by the bucketful. Power now came from the "long-block" development of the Colombo V12 as seen in the 330 GT 2+2, while for the 330 GTB its four liters, with three carbs, gave a lazy and sophisticated 300bhp. And that's what the 330s were all about: lazy.

Above *1969 Ferrari 365 GTC, Chas. No 12449*

Below
top *Lamborghini Miura*
bottom *Turin Show 1965. "Miura", the new Lamborghini, clearly showing transverse engine layout, with 4 triple choke Webers feeding the 12 cylinders*

sophisticated performance for an ever more sophisticated market. It meant that a 330 GTB or GTS, with a maximum nearing 150mph, was no faster than the similarly powerful four-cam 275 GTB/4 (or the very rare GTS/4 Spyders, built for US importer Luigi Chinetti) but much more flexible in the middle ranges, and because it was rather lower revving it was a lot more relaxing for the average driver—even a Ferrari driver.

An effortless cruiser

In one way, this was how the Ferrari character, and the Ferrari market, was developing, yet however much the late 1960s generation of Ferrari customers liked their creature comforts, poise was nothing without performance. That led, inevitably, to the next development, the 365 family, led by the 365 California in 1966 (as described in Chapter 4) and then the 365 GT 2+2 in 1967.

The California was short-lived. With its solid axle and non-independent rear suspension it was, strictly speaking, out of the series in the same way that the 330 GT 2+2 had been, but the 365 GT 2+2 was a different animal altogether, one of Ferrari's more under-rated "family" alternatives. Pininfarina styled and built it, of course, its long, slightly drooping tail and fiddly rear window line were a bit out of character, but overall it looked like a Ferrari and, in spite of its size and its ability to genuinely carry two small or flexible adults in the back, it went like one. By increasing the bore of the 4-liter two-cam 330 engine, Ferrari had pushed capacity up to 4.4 liters and power up to 320bhp. That gave a top speed of more than 150mph with plenty of off-the-line acceleration for such a big, relatively heavy and luxuriously equipped vehicle. But its main strength was its effortless mid-range performance, backed up by almost unrivaled high-speed cruising ability and one other new dimension: amazingly, this was the first Ferrari 2+2 to offer all-independent suspension, and that transformed it.

There were, of course, 365 alternatives for the customer who wanted something a bit more compact and visibly sporty. They were the 365 GTC and 365 GTS, built between the end of 1968 and, in the case of the GTC, at least the beginning of 1970, although the GTS was gone by early 1969. These 365s were easy to recognize as a continuation of the similar 330 GT models, Coupé and Spyder. They looked almost identical, and mechanically the only big difference was 4.4 liters instead of 4 liters and 320bhp instead of 300bhp, with performance edging ahead again, and now comfortably over 150mph.

The ultimate grand tourer

Remarkably, this was no longer enough. Ferrari still had competition, and by the time Enzo came to launch his next major flagship model, in 1968, someone had changed the rules The man from Sant'Agata had done it again, and Ferrari was right in the firing line.

In 1966, Lamborghini blew the supercar world apart again when he launched one of the most dramatic sportscars of all time, the incredible Miura. It started life with a 4-liter V12 and

Below *1973 Ferrari 365 GTB/4 Daytona and engine detail showing the six twin-choke downdraft Weber carburetors that helped to produce a massive 352bhp*

Below left *The interior of a 1971 Daytona*

***Above** 1974 Ferrari 365 GTS/4 Daytona Spyder, conversion by Autokraft*

350bhp, but the most sensational thing about the Miura was that it was mid-engined—the first mid-engined supercar the world had ever seen.

This was not something Ferrari was really ready for. He already built mid-engined Grand Prix models, of course, and mid-engined sports racers, but in both areas he had been among the last on the grid to make the change, and he was going to be just as stubborn with his road designs. By the time Lamborghini showed the Miura, Ferrari had been building mid-engined competition automobiles for more than five years without ever showing a sign of transferring the layout to the road. It was 1965 before a mid-engined Ferrari road prototype even appeared as a concept, and that was just a Pininfarina exercise, unveiled at the Paris Show that October. It was called the Dino, and although the Dino 206 GT went into production in the middle of 1968, it was a much smaller car than Lamborghini's Miura, and strictly speaking wasn't even called a Ferrari.

When Enzo did come to creating the vehicle to regain the supercar crown from the Miura, he was going to do it his way—the traditional way. The front-engined layout would raise eyebrows, but it wouldn't stop this particular Ferrari from being one of the greatest of them all, one of the greatest supercars of any era from any manufacturer.

It was introduced at the Paris Show in October 1968 under the designation 365 GTB/4, otherwise known as the Daytona. It was the most expensive production Ferrari ever built, and the fastest. Faster, in fact, than the Miura—and whether Ferrari would admit it or not, in 1968 that was what mattered most.

The Daytona name came from the Florida racing venue, and Ferrari's many successes there in endurance racing; the 365 was the pointer to the capacity, 4.4 liters; the GTB stood for Gran Turismo Berlinetta; and the 4 was the radical part, for four camshafts. This was perhaps the greatest Ferrari production engine to date, and is still reckoned to be one of the greatest more than 30 years on. It was built around a new version of an old starting point: Lampredi's big short-stroke long-block V12. With all-new cylinder heads, each carrying a pair of chain-driven overhead camshafts, it was a mighty engine in every respect. It had six twin-choke downdraught Weber carburetors and produced a massive 352bhp. It was hardly a coincidence that that was two more than the Miura at the time.

But that glorious engine was only the start of what made the Daytona so special. In 1970 it also appeared in the successor to the 365 2+2, the 365 GTC/4. Detuned to "only" 320bhp and in the far less muscular-looking 2+2 shape, it was good (and a big seller with around 500 built) but it was no Daytona rival. In fact, in its day, nothing, Ferrari or otherwise, rivaled the fantastic 365 GTB/4.

It looked huge, but it actually sat on the same wheelbase as the elegant 275 GTB/4, and although it was a little bigger overall, and a little heavier, it wasn't by much. The power was up by such a huge leap that the Daytona could boast a power-to-weight ratio of 200bhp per ton—a monster figure for 1968, and big even now. That gave the Daytona a maximum speed, independently tested, of 174mph, which made it the fastest car in the world, period. Moreover, the 365 GTB/4 V12 had so much pulling power everywhere through the rev range that the mighty Daytona could accelerate to 60mph in less than 5.5 seconds, and to 100mph in just over 12.5 seconds—all figures that still qualify for the big-hitter league in the twenty-first century.

But even that wasn't all. With the Daytona, however unlikely it seemed to anybody who thought modern had to mean mid-engined, Ferrari proved that a front-engined GT could still be one of the finest handling cars in the world. This was front-engined with all Ferrari's unrivaled experience and flair. The Daytona came about as close to perfect front-to-rear balance as it is possible to go. The engine was set as far back in the chassis as it could sit and, as in the 275, the five-speed transmission was split from the engine as a rear transaxle. Its Pininfarina styling—long, high-fronted, short, crop-tailed and crouched wide and low on the biggest five-spoke alloy wheels and the most rubber that could be crammed into the swooping wheel arches—was eloquent of how the Daytona drove. It was an athlete, a bare-knuckle fighter, a long-distance runner, a sprinter. Every superlative rolled into one. On real roads it was unequalled for massive mile-crunching muscle allied to fantastic usability. It was a true grand tourer, reasonable on luggage space, refined and in a league of its own for pure character. It was even quite comfortable, beautifully trimmed and surprisingly well equipped.

In 1969, Ferrari went a stage further and introduced a Daytona Spyder. It was a hell of a way to go soft-top motoring, but where Ferrari built some 1,285 coupés, he only made 127 Spyders, and although they became one of the most expensive automobiles in the world in later years, the real classic is still the coupé.

When it finally went out of production, in 1974, it marked the end of an era. Its replacement would bow to progress and have the engine placed behind the driver—ironically attracting the criticism that Ferrari had gone backwards, that the new model wasn't as good as the old one. The simple fact was, the Daytona was a very tough act to follow.

Above *1973 Ferrari Daytona*

Below *1971 Ferrari 365 GTC/4, Chas. No 15709, and very original*

The Dino and Beyond

Up to the late 1960s, Enzo Ferrari had never built a series production road automobile with fewer than a dozen cylinders, or with its engine anywhere other than in front of the driver. Certainly he had built racing cars with engine layouts other than his favourite, the classic V12. In fact, he'd tried most options, including four cylinders, six cylinders and eight cylinders, in lines and in vees. Grudgingly, for the racetrack he had already started to put the engine behind the driver; for the road, though, Ferrari had stuck stubbornly with the formula he'd adopted right from the start: twelve cylinders, up front.

Unfortunately, by the late 1960s, seduced by motor racing (and by the dramatic arrival of Lamborghini as a builder of super-exotic road models), some of the supercar-buying public saw engines in the middle as the future, and engines in front as things of the past. This put Ferrari in a spot, not because he couldn't design and engineer a perfectly fine mid-engined roadster, but because he didn't want to. It had taken Enzo years to bow to progress in motor racing. For a road model he didn't see a mid-engine as progress at all. The layout had its handling advantages, but they came with too many compromises for a car which had to be usable and practical. For the average driver, it would present too much of a challenge at the vehicle's limits. For the grand tourer, it would make it too short on space and visibility. Ferrari wasn't interested in fashion; he would leave that to Lamborghini. Ferrari was interested in classic engineering, and tradition. And once he made up his mind, no one was likely to change it.

Dino's V6

Or virtually no one. There was one person he did listen to, someone Enzo felt he could learn from, because he would be improved by the dialog, not tricked by it. The one person Ferrari could accept ideas from without feeling he was sacrificing his soul wasn't one of his legendary engineers, it was his own son, Dino (see box on p. 73).

In fact, Dino had died in 1956, aged just 24. His father spent the rest of his life mourning him. Dino had been ill for most of his short life but had spent as much time as he could working with his father, especially discussing ideas. His most far-reaching idea, and the one his father took up with such relish and always thought of as Dino's great legacy, was the idea of the compact V6 engine.

Previous page *1974 Ferrari Dino 246 GTS*

Below
left *Dino 246 engines being assembled at Maranello in 1973*
right *The Pininfarina Dino Berlinetta Speciale at the Paris Show 1965*

Dino Ferrari: the Son Who Died

On June 30 1956 Dino Ferrari passed away, and Enzo Ferrari's life changed for ever. Dino was Enzo's only legitimate son. When he died, Ferrari mourned for the rest of his life. Not only had he lost the son he loved, he had lost an heir. Enzo honoured his memory with the Dino series of V6 racing engines and the road cars which followed. The depth of his feeling is revealed in the introduction to his 1963 autobiography, *My Terrible Joys*, dedicated to Dino. Ferrari wrote: "In recent years I have been asked on more than one occasion to write the story of my life. Until now I have never fallen in with the suggestion . . . But the death of my son induced me to pause sadly and reflect. Catching my breath, I looked back down the long road I have travelled. With my life stretched away behind me I decided to find release in this dialog with myself, hoping it was not too late; a dialog in solitude, in the shadow of the greatest sorrow of my life."

Enzo Ferrari had married Laura in the early 1920s. Their son was born on 19 January 1932, christened Alfredo and nicknamed Alfredino, or "little Alfredo" which was soon shortened to Dino. Enzo was devoted to Dino and obviously saw in him a successor to the Ferrari heritage. Unlike Enzo, Dino received some formal technical training. He studied at the Corni Technical Institute in Modena and by correspondence at the University of Fribourg in Switzerland. He also studied economics and commerce at Bologna University. He was clearly being groomed for a big future.

He spent much of his young life around the factory, talking with his father, but Dino was frequently ill. He had developed muscular dystrophy, and there was no cure, only the prospect of growing progressively weaker until death came. Dino apparently found that easier to accept than his father, and was known to all who knew him as a cheerful and friendly young man, unfailingly helpful and ever eager to learn and to talk.

His interest in all that happened in the factory, and especially in the racing department, was what led to the V6 racing engine being credited to him. Dino had driven some minor races with a succession of small Fiats, but as a Ferrari driver he had been limited to testing the 2-liter sports cars. Dino loved motor sport, but Enzo was very protective. He continued, however, to talk with his father and the engineers, even as his illness progressed, and although the majority of design work for that first Ferrari V6 was completed by Vittorio Jano, it is clear that Ferrari had decided Dino should have his memorial. As he wrote in his memoirs, "his last work was done in the long and snowy winter in which his ailment, a nephritis virus, kept him almost constantly confined to his bed. I and my old friend Jano spent long hours at his bedside, discussing with him the design of a 1.5-liter engine . . . I remember how carefully and with what competence Dino read and discussed all the notes and reports that were brought to him daily from Maranello. For reasons of mechanical efficiency, he finally came to the conclusion that the engine should be a V6, and we accepted this decision. There was thus born the famous 156, which was to burst into song for the first time in November 1956, five months after Dino had passed away."

After his death, Ferrari was totally distraught. Enzo left Dino's office at the factory exactly as it had been the last time Dino used it, with a photograph on the chair where he used to sit. For years afterwards Ferrari visited Dino's grave every day, and often spent time talking to him about particular problems.

What Dino might have achieved had he lived we will never know. Neither can we know if Fiat would have taken a major interest in Ferrari in the late 1960s had Dino been holding the reins of the company. What is interesting to remember, though, is that it was the success of the Dino engine and the road model Ferrari designed around it that prompted the dramatic growth of the company, and the original Fiat involvement. Perhaps, at the end of the day, that is Dino's real legacy.

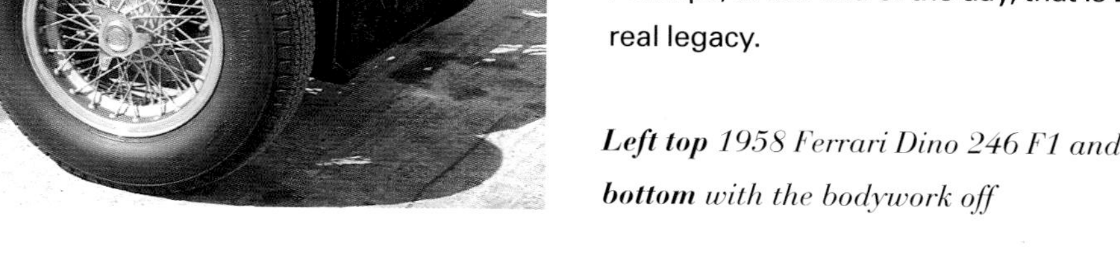

Left top *1958 Ferrari Dino 246 F1 and* ***bottom*** *with the bodywork off*

Dino had proposed it originally for a racing role, for the new Formula Two regulations of the late 1950s, although he didn't actually do much beyond suggesting the basic layout and supporting the man who really designed it, the brilliant Vittorio Jano. The engine first ran just before Dino died, and soon after it became hugely successful in the formula it was designed for, Formula Two. Later, Enzo adopted his son's compact V6 layout for the new Formula One, for sportscar racing and for hillclimbing, in each case with success. Later still, with Lancia, a "Dino" V6 even became a multiple world rally champion. But beyond its role in racing, Dino's V6 configuration had another life—in the first mid-engined, non-V12 Ferrari production road model.

Still, for Enzo it wasn't as simple as just building the vehicle. There were commercial and sporting considerations beyond the family background. When Dino conceived the first V6 Formula Two engine in the mid-1950s, it could be built purely as a racing engine, in tiny numbers. By the mid-1960s that had all changed, and things were more complicated. According to the rules of the day, to qualify a version of the latest Dino V6 for Formula Two racing 1960s style, it had to be based on a "production" engine of which at least 500 had been built in one year. At the time, Ferrari's total annual production barely reached 700. Even in a small model which could have been sold for rather less than his usual products, Ferrari couldn't hope to achieve so many sales in so short a time.

Instead, he formed a partnership with Italian motor industry giant Fiat, who would build the V6 on Ferrari's behalf and use a version of it in a reasonably affordable production sports model (or, rather, two) of their own. These cars were the front-engined Fiat Dinos introduced in November 1966, a decade after Dino's death, as a Pininfarina-bodied Spyder or a Bertone-bodied coupé. The engine, the third generation of the Dino V6 but the first intended for road as well as track, was an all-alloy four-cam unit with a capacity of two liters.

***Right** 1967 Ferrari Dino 206 Pininfarina (2) Competizione. There were two versions of this concept, the first having a different tail*

The badgeless Dinos

The Fiat Dinos were interesting, effective and successful, but they weren't the most exciting roadgoing home for the Ferrari V6. In 1968, with the Fiat Dino well established and the Dino 166 F2 proving its point on the racetrack, Ferrari launched a Dino for the road. Not only did it have six cylinders, but the engine was behind the driver.

It had started life as a Pininfarina styling exercise, the Dino Berlinetta, at the Paris Show in October 1965. In November 1966 a second version, the Dino Berlinetta GT, had appeared at the Turin Show. A year later, in Turin again, Pininfarina had shown what turned out to be an almost production-ready third version. Finally, in the middle of 1968, Ferrari launched his first mid-engined production automobile, and laid the foundations for a new line of more compact designs which, through models like the 246 GT, the 308 GTB, the 328 and 348, still has echoes in the glorious 360 more than 30 years after Ferrari took the mid-engined plunge.

But in the beginning there was a piece of classic Enzo Ferrari awkwardness. It wasn't difficult to see that this was one of the most significant cars Ferrari had ever made, not only because of its new layout but also because, potentially, as a far more affordable and accessible car than the big V12 grand tourers, it could take Ferrari into a bigger market than he had ever reached so far. But however hard you looked, you wouldn't have found either the Ferrari name or the prancing horse emblem anywhere on its body.

The new version was called the Dino 206 GT, and by naming it that way Ferrari was being very shrewd, even by his own standards. Of course, he would say, the name honored his dead son, who had conceived the idea of the V6 engine. But at the same time, calling the car a Dino left Enzo a useful escape route to silence any "big" Ferrari owner, or potential owner, who might say that a small Ferrari, or any with fewer than a dozen cylinders, devalued the name. This may sound bizarre now, but that was how Ferrari's mind could work.By any name, and no matter that it came in a smaller package, the Dino 206 GT was a great automobile, and the start of a great line which would eventually become Ferrari in name as well as character.

Top *Ferrari Dino 206 GT. The 206 can be distinguished from the later 246 by the exposed fuel filler cap and knock-on wheels*

Above *Dino assembly at the Scaglietti plant, 1973*

Above and right *Interior and engine bay, 1973 Ferrari Dino 246 GT*

Opposite page *How to style a classic: whatever the angle Pininfarina always seems to get it just right*

The 206 tag represented an alternative Ferrari numbering system, not the capacity of a single cylinder but the overall capacity (in this case two liters) plus the number of cylinders (six). The four-cam V6, with a vee angle of 65 degrees rather than the classic V12's 60 degrees, was a more highly tuned version than the one in the Fiat Dinos, and with three downdraught Weber carburetors it produced a healthy 180bhp. In such a light, compact design, that gave performance which not so long ago wouldn't have been out of place in Ferrari's big V12s, and in its day would frighten virtually any other 2-liter production model, including those from new arch rival Porsche. In fact, a top speed of around 145mph and 0–60mph in not much more than seven seconds is pretty quick for a 2-liter car even today—and, of course, the 206 GT added a new dimension with its brilliant handling and sheer usability.

It was all in the compact packaging and the subtly different character of the mid-engined layout. By normal Ferrari standards the Dino was both small and light. In the first show design, the 1965 Paris version, the engine sat longitudinally behind the driver and ahead of the transmission and rear axle. The same layout was repeated in the 1966 Turin Show model, but by 1967, and the third version, the engine had been turned around to sit transversely, which is how it appeared in the road version. The transmission was still behind, but now in effect alongside the V6 block, so the whole arrangement was more compact and better balanced, with as much weight as possible concentrated in the middle . It also meant there was room for a reasonable luggage compartment at the back, in addition to what could be squeezed under the short and low front hood, around the spare wheel. And the Dino's all-wishbone, all-independent suspension, disk brakes all round, and generously sized alloy wheels created a brilliant handling package.

The all-alloy body, styled by Pininfarina and built by Scaglietti, was every bit as attractive as the mechanical specification, and it's a tribute to how good it was in 1968 that it still looks good

WWB 645L

today. The proportions were beautiful, and so were Pininfarina's answers to feeding air into (and out of) the mid-engine—the lovely deep side vents and the distinctive "'lying buttress" rear window.

Good as the Dino 206 GT was, and enthusiastically received as it turned out to be, Ferrari didn't build many of the original—probably around 150 vehicles before production ended late in 1969. But that was just the beginning for the small Ferrari. The 206 GT was replaced immediately by the 246 GT, and although that had a few more compromises than the 206, it was a more user-friendly automobile, and commercially was massively more successful.

The biggest difference was a virtually all-new engine, to overcome the valve gear and cylinder head reliability problems of the original. It wasn't quite so exotic, though, because now that it needed to be built in even bigger numbers but no longer had to be adaptable for racing it was given a cast-iron block rather than an aluminum one. That made it heavier, and it changed the balance of the car slightly, but pushing capacity up to 2.4 liters more than made up for the extra weight with more power and a lot more flexibility. Output was now 195bhp, and the 246 was at least as quick as a 206 at top speed and in a 0–60mph dash, and mainly quicker in the most important middle-range acceleration figures. That made it an easier car to drive lazily, without having to stir the wonderfully slick five-speed transmission quite so much if you weren't in the mood.

In spite of a small increase in wheelbase and a switch from alloy bodies to steel, the looks had changed very little, because they didn't need to. Indeed, they wouldn't change through the 246 GT's five-year production run. What did change, in 1970, was that Ferrari added a second version. The targa-topped 246 GTS wasn't the traditional soft-topped spyder, but it did offer a choice: open-topped motoring by removing the rigid center roof panel. So even if it was still badged Dino, the 'small' Ferrari had made the grade, big time.

__Below__ 1978 Ferrari 308 GT/4 2+2. This is a rare design, being Bertone's only road-going production automobile since the 1950s. Announced in 1973 as a Dino, the name and badges were changed to Ferrari in 1976

Above 1980 Ferrari 308 GTS

Collaboration with Fiat

As well as changing the look of the designs, the Dino helped change the face of Ferrari the company. In 1960, the old Auto Avio Costruzione had given way to Società Esercizio Fabbriche Automobili e Corse (SEFAC) Ferrari, combining the production and racing activities under one new corporate name for the first time. In its five years on sale, Ferrari would build more than 3,000 of the 246 generation, and that led to a new kind of production operation, one bigger than Ferrari himself had ever dreamed when he was forming the company, probably even until the Dino generation was born.

To handle it, he added a new 100,000-square-foot production area to the Maranello works. Even more importantly, in 1969 he relinquished a 50 percent share of the company to Fiat. Far from being a step backwards, it was one of Enzo Ferrari's finest moves. Fiat would take control of building the road models while guaranteeing major, long-term backing for Ferrari's racing activities, and Enzo would be allowed to stay in absolute control of the racing side for as long as he wished, which so far as he was concerned meant for as long as he had breath in his body. It was an arrangement that suited both sides very well indeed, and if there had been one catalyst for it, it was these first Dinos.

Burgeoning Dino production

In 1974, Ferrari followed up the 246 GT and GTS family with another newcomer, the Dino 308 GT/4, which had actually been unveiled in Paris towards the end of 1973. It was a mid-engined 2+2, and was the first Ferrari road model to use a V8 engine, but few people understood where it was going.

For one thing, it was the first road-going Ferrari in years not to come from the pen of Pininfarina. It was styled by Bertone, and its angular lines were very different from the beautiful

***Below** 1981 Ferrari 308 GTSi interior*

curves of the 206 and 246 V6s. At the time, in looks at least, hardly anybody thought it was a step forward, but it did have more power and performance, and looking back on it now, Bertone actually did a clever job of making the difficult mid-engined 2+2 layout look neat and sporty.

To compensate for the inevitably increased weight, and also for the more stringent emissions regulations that were starting to be pushed on to the whole industry, the all-alloy four-cam V8 took capacity to three liters (hence 308) and power output to 250bhp. With that, the 308 could top 150mph and push seven seconds to 60mph, which was big performance for a compact 2+2, matched by a still impressive chassis that, in spite of its longer wheelbase, kept a lot of the nimbleness, feedback and character of the earlier Dinos.

None of which, unfortunately, made the market love it, although enough people wanted to buy it for it to survive until 1980, and to sell more than 3,000 copies—more than the 246. It didn't even help the image particularly when Ferrari finally put his badge on the Bertone 308, along with the Dino ones. It was just that sort of car.

Fortunately for Ferrari's credibility, by 1978, for anyone who really wanted a 308, it wasn't the only game in town. At the 1975 Paris Show, Ferrari gave them what they wanted in the 308 GTB. The GTB—and its inevitable spin-off, the 308 GTS, launched in 1977—was a very different car from the GT/4. It was styled by Pininfarina, had at least hints of the old Dino look, especially at the back, and people loved it just as much as they hated Bertone's GT/4. They didn't even seem to mind that the GTB was the first Ferrari to have a fiberglass body—

Below *1980s Ferrari 208 GTS Turbo. It was introduced to benefit from low Italian sales tax on cars with an engine capacity under 2 liters. The car is distinguishable from a standard 308 by a roof spoiler, slats in the front hood panel and NACA ducts in the flanks, similar to those in a 512 BB (these not visible in this shot)*

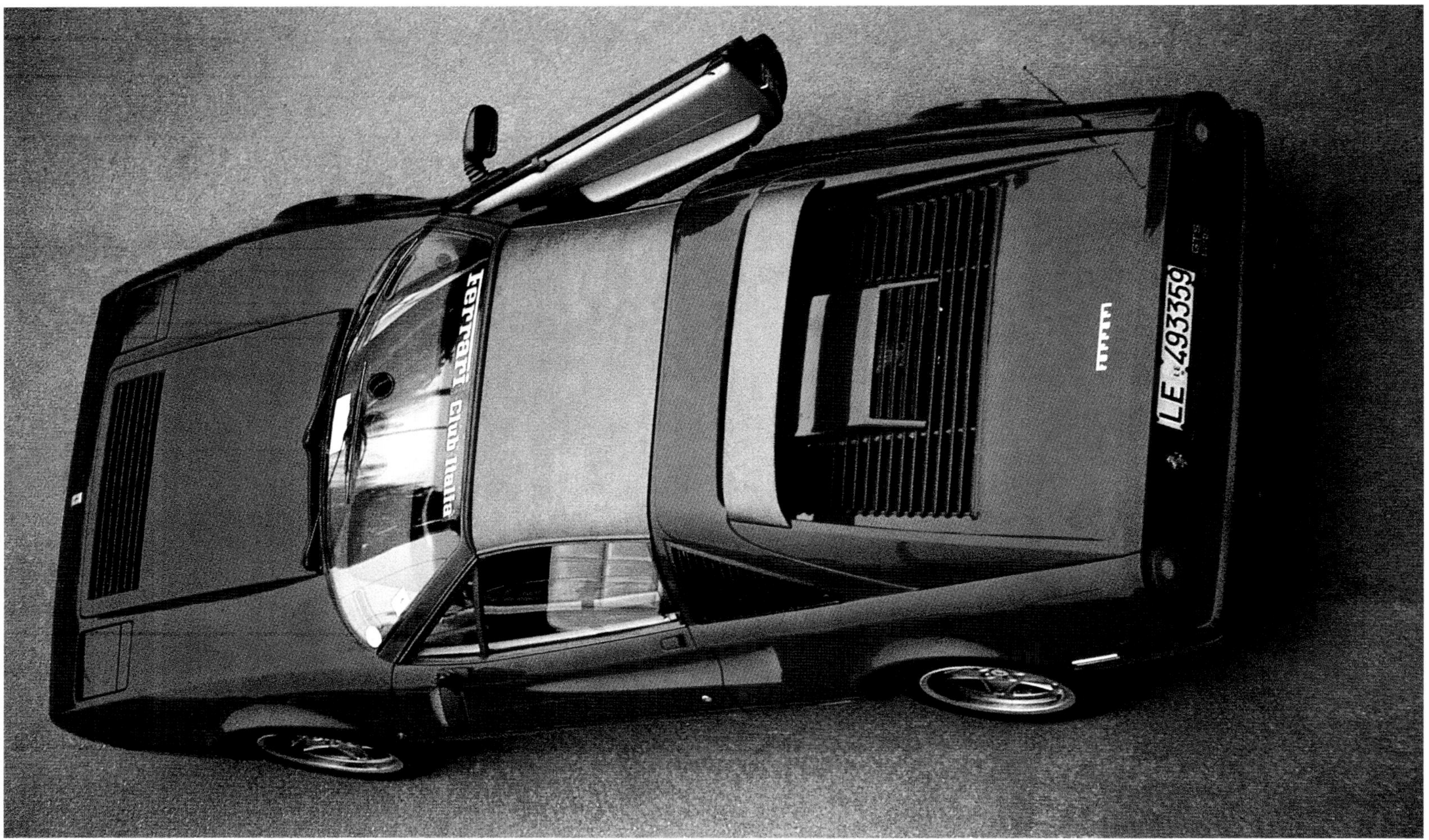

The Dino's First Cousins

The real catalyst for the Fiat Dinos was the need to make up the production numbers to enable Ferrari's version of the V6 Dino engine to go racing, but the V6 Fiats were interesting cars in their own right.

The first version was unveiled at the Turin Show in 1966, bright red and styled by Pininfarina, but a Fiat, not a Ferrari. This was the Fiat Dino Spyder, and under the shapely hood was Fiat's production version of the Dino engine, which would also power the Ferrari-built Dino road models and become a major success as a racing engine. The first version of the Fiat engine had all-alloy construction, four overhead camshafts and a capacity of just two liters. Ferrari's original version, with a higher state of tune and different jets in the carburetors, would produce 180bhp; the Fiat version was essentially the same, but to keep production costs down it was less highly tuned, made do with less extreme carburetion, and gave 160bhp. At least, those were supposed to be the respective power outputs. A lot of people thought the real difference was probably a lot smaller, and the quoted numbers had more to do with politics than engineering. Even so, 160bhp was enough to make the Dino Spyder the fastest Fiat you could buy at the time, with a maximum speed of over 120mph—nothing spectacular for a 1966 Ferrari, but quite something for a 1966 Fiat, and a roadster at that.

More important than the possibly minor differences in the engines themselves was the difference in the way they were mounted. Ferrari put the V6 transversely in the back of their Dino, Fiat mounted it longitudinally in the front of theirs—which again was a useful way of making the Ferrari version acceptably more exotic. The Fiat was in other respects, too, entirely conventional, with a five-speed manual transmission behind the engine, driving the rear wheels.

Mechanically, the Fiat Dino Coupé, launched in 1967, was almost identical to the Spyder except for the fact that it sat on a noticeably longer wheelbase, to make room for reasonably roomy 2+2 seating. Both platforms were made by Fiat, but where the two-door, two-seat Spyder was styled and bodied by Pininfarina, the two-door fastback 2+2 Coupé was styled and bodied by Bertone. Beyond the rooflines, the two versions looked completely different in most respects save that both used a fashionable four-headlight layout.

The Fiats could sell in much bigger numbers than the Ferrari-built Dinos because they were simpler to build and substantially cheaper, partly because they were made in much bigger numbers, and partly because they borrowed a number of components (even quite major assemblies) from other Fiat production models. The suspension, for example, was based on that of the 125 sedan, while the brakes, steering and lots of minor components, seen and unseen, came straight from the Fiat production parts bin.

Nonetheless, they were very expensive Fiats and were only saleable because they really were quite good sporty models. The quality of the engine went without saying (although it did have some reliability problems, especially with cylinder head gaskets), but what surprised most people was how good the chassis was, even though it had nothing more exotic than leaf springs and a live axle at the back, just like the Ferraris of old but hardly leading edge at the time.

They changed when the Ferrari-built Dinos changed, to adopt the later 2.4-liter version of the V6—which gave the Dino the new designation 246 GT and the Fiats the additional tag 2400. This was the iron-blocked engine, which on paper wasn't quite so exotic but in practice was easier to build, more reliable and more powerful. In Fiat spec it took quoted power up to where Ferrari's Dino had started, 180bhp, while the Ferrari version jumped to 195bhp. As well as upping top speed to comfortably over 130mph in the Fiats, with markedly better acceleration to match, the new versions also gained independent rear suspension and many other detail changes.

In many ways they were even better than the first versions, but they had long ago done their original job of qualifying the Dino V6 engine for motor sport, so they didn't survive for much longer. By the time production stopped, in 1973, the total built had just passed 7,500—around two and a half times as many Dinos as Ferrari had made in the same time.

Top *1968 Fiat Dino Spyder 2.0 liter* ***Middle*** *Fiat Dino Coupé 2.4* ***Bottom*** *Fiat Dino engine*

***Above** 1982 Ferrari Mondial Quattrovalvole*

until the GTS prompted Pininfarina to revert to steel bodies, because with the roof gone the spyder needed the extra stiffness. The fact that, in terms of power, performance and on-road character there was actually little difference between the GT/4 and the GTB (or GTS), showed just how fickle the market could be. Even Ferrari had to tread carefully. But with Pininfarina back in the equation and now, finally, with the Ferrari name on the front, the 308 GTB and GTS were big winners.

Selling initially alongside the Bertone-bodied 308 GT/4, the Pininfarina models outsold it in a big way, and significantly, in spite of soft-tops having a few problems in a safety-obsessed US market, the GTS Spyder versions over the whole production run (which lasted up to 1985) outsold the coupés by almost two to one: just over 8,000 Spyders against not quite 4,150 Berlinettas. Either way, these were now very serious production numbers, and Ferrari under Fiat was growing quite dramatically.

The designs, too, continued to evolve. For some European markets with tax advantages for smaller capacities, between 1975 and 1983 Ferrari offered 2-liter spin-offs from the range in all three body styles, as the 208 GT/4, the 208 GTB, and the 208 GTS. And if the 170bhp 2-liter models weren't exciting enough, from 1982 to 1985 Ferrari added turbocharged 208 GTB and GTS models, with another 50bhp and just about enough performance to live with the 3-liter 308s.

Or maybe not quite, because as time went on the 308 also evolved. First, in 1980, the V8 was given fuel injection, not so much to increase power (which it didn't) as to cling on to it as emissions regulations became tougher still. In fact, the first injected versions, badged 308 GTBi (and GTSi, of course), had lost a good (or bad) 40bhp or so in European spec, and even more in US trim. That obviously did nothing for performance, but it wasn't just a Ferrari problem, it was the same for everybody. In 1982, while still improving emissions performance, Ferrari clawed at least some of it back with the next development for the 3-liter V8 family, four-valve cylinder heads, which brought another new designation: 308 GTBqv (and GTSqv), for "*quattrovalvole*", or four valves.

To complete this part of the story, there was one other variation in the 308 line which was always the homely cousin but which, with hindsight, stands out as a much cleverer vehicle than many people recognized at the time. It was the model which, in 1980, finally replaced Bertone's 'four-seater' 308 GTB/4. It was another 2+2—that was the whole point—it was styled by Pininfarina but looked a lot squarer than the curvy GTB and GTS, and in its first version it was called the Mondial 8. It arrived with the fuel-injected two-valve generation of the 3-liter V8, and around 215bhp. Aside from a slightly stretched wheelbase and a taller roofline, it had most of the chassis detail of the two-seaters and genuinely offered a very decent compromise between worthwhile rear seats, surprising comfort and refinement, and the real Ferrari driving experience. In 1982, in line with its 308 cousins, it became the Mondial qv and, almost inevitably, from 1983 there was a cabriolet version.

You could argue for a very long time about whether the Mondial was a better-looking car than the GTB/4, or whether it was really any better to drive, but it was certainly more popular—in truth, probably because it was by now more completely thought out as a practical, comfortable, easy to live with "family" car. As such, it was another interesting string to the Dino family's bow.

Left *1984 Ferrari Mondial Cabriolet Quattrovalvole. Early examples had leaky roofs, and with the hood down, turbulence was enormous, but it was a Ferrari you could fit the children in, and it still sounded right!*

The Mid-engined Flagships

However you look at it, Enzo Ferrari didn't believe in doing things by the book—at least, not other people's books. By 1973, virtually all his rivals in the supercar world topped their ranges with a mid-engined design; some, like Porsche, didn't have a model at all with the engine in the front. But even after he'd bitten the mid-engined bullet back in 1968 with the launch of the Dino, when it came to producing a "full-sized" Ferrari with the engine in the back, Enzo held back.

The Countach and the Boxer

In 1973, though, he faced the moment of truth, the moment when he couldn't avoid the inevitable any longer. Arch rival Ferrucio Lamborghini may have been in business for less than a decade but he, possibly more than anyone else, had been giving Ferrari something to think about—not only in terms of sales success but also with the company's amazingly high profile. From the moment Lamborghini had launched into the supercar business it had grabbed the headlines, not least with the sensational Miura, launched in 1966, an automobile to rival any of the big Ferraris for power, performance, and sophistication. Two years before Ferrari had even introduced the compact 2-liter V6 Dino, the 4-liter V12-powered Miura was pointedly mid-engined. By 1971, Lamborghini had already shown off the prototype of the Miura's mid-engined successor, the even more spectacular Countach, and Ferrari still hadn't gone down the big mid-engine route.

By the time the Countach prototype appeared, he was at least thinking about it, and not long after the clues to the next big-league Lamborghini had been revealed, Ferrari showed a prototype of his own. He unveiled it at the Turin Show in 1971, and it was clear that this was likely to be a replacement for the Daytona. It was a Pininfarina-styled concept labeled the BB, which stood for 'Berlinetta Boxer' and revealed the first bit of new thinking.

Previous page *1990 Ferrari Testarossa*

Below *1971 Lamborghini Countach Concept, shown at launch at the Geneva Show*

Right *Pininfarina Ferrari Boxer on display at the 1971 Turin Show*

__Above__ May 1973, the Fiorano test track pits. Left to right: Col Ronnie Hoare (owner of Maranello Concessionaires, the UK Ferrari dealership), Enzo Ferrari and Andrea Catanzano, the development engineer, pose with prototype Ferrari 365 Boxer

The "Berlinetta" part was familiar enough, Ferrari-speak for a closed design; the "Boxer" was new, and referred to an all-new engine layout. It was a major revolution for Ferrari whichever end of the car it had been at—or at least a major revolution as far as a Ferrari road model was concerned, because by this time the Boxer configuration had been Ferrari's layout of choice, on and off, for their Grand Prix and prototype sportscar racing engines for almost ten years. It referred to a horizontally opposed or "flat" cylinder arrangement, with the pistons "boxing" each other. Citroën used it with two cylinders in the 2CV, Volkswagen used it with four cylinders in the Beetle, and Porsche used it with six in the 911. Naturally, Ferrari's Boxer engine would use twelve cylinders. Another way of looking at it would be as a V12 with a 180-degree vee angle.

Ferrari could no longer avoid his flagship production car reflecting what customers on this level saw as the ultimate, race-bred technology—which also, of course, included putting the engine behind the driver. Whether all this was actually an advantage for a road design was another question, and largely immaterial. The market knew best, and if Ferrari wouldn't build what they wanted, someone else would.

So that was the BB concept: a flat-12 engine, mid-mounted, in a strictly two-seater coupé whose styling was a spectacular step ahead for Ferrari but actually looked quite low-key alongside Lamborghini's outrageous newcomer, the Countach. Technically, however, it involved some very exciting thinking—Ferrari's way of answering the same problems Lamborghini had already been faced with. Foremost among them was how to find room for a dozen cylinders—which inevitably means a pretty long engine, even before you add the transmission—behind the driver and still end up with reasonable interior space in an acceptably compact design.

Lamborghini's answer, with the Miura, had been similar to Ferrari's with the much smaller Dino: to mount the engine transversely, which required a considerably greater miracle of packaging for the V12 Lamborghini than it had for the V6-engined Ferrari. For the Miura, Lamborghini had also found a novel solution to the other thorny part of the problem: where to squeeze the transmission. They copied the Mini, and put it into the bottom of the engine, in effect into the oil pan. As in the Mini, it was a brilliant piece of packaging, but having the engine and transmission sharing the same oil wasn't quite as satisfactory in the 350bhp Miura as it was in the 32bhp Mini. If you tried to make the oil last too long, the engine wouldn't. In the even more powerful later versions, Lamborghini separated the two oil systems, but when they designed the Countach, they came up with another solution altogether.

In the Countach, the massive V12 was located longitudinally, and the equally massive transmission was "conventionally" mounted on the end of it, making one hugely long assembly. The clever bit was that Lamborghini put their transmission in front instead of behind the engine, and squeezed it forwards into the cabin, between driver and passenger in the big center tunnel. They then ran power back to the final drive via a shaft running literally *through* the engine, alongside the crankshaft. It was still a very large piece of engineering, but the brilliantly unconventional layout made the Countach almost compact.

With the BB, however, Ferrari adopted yet another layout, with its own advantages and disadvantages. With the flat-12 configuration the engine was reasonably, well, flat, but it was almost as wide as it was long, leaving no advantage in fitting it in transversely. So Ferrari chose

Right *Early 365 Boxer engine on the test bed at Maranello, 1973*

Above 1974 Ferrari 365 GTB/4/BB

to mount the Boxer engine longitudinally, ahead of the rear axle line, putting the five-speed transmission below the crankshaft and the final drive behind it. Again, it was a very clever exercise in getting a quart into a pint pot, the main drawback being that it forced the considerable weight of the engine rather further off the ground than Ferrari would have liked, so the center of gravity at the back was higher than would have been ideal.

On the whole, though, it was a good compromise. By mounting the radiator and other weighty bits in the longish front end, Ferrari could keep the front-to-rear weight distribution something close to balanced while avoiding most of the problems the side-radiatored Lamborghini Countach had with cooling, which meant its original, clean shape was soon complicated by tack-on ducts. The BB production model, not just BB the concept, never had to resort to remedies as messy as that.

The Boxer launch

The production model was officially launched at the Paris Show in 1973, as the 365 GTB/4/BB. Save for the 'BB' part, the model number was just the same as the design it replaced, the legendary Daytona. But beyond the numbers the similarities were few. The BB had the same capacity as the Daytona, 4.4 liters from the same bore and stroke dimensions, so it could use the same pistons and connecting rods, but it didn't inherit much else. The crankshaft and block were obviously totally different with the flat layout. The four camshafts were driven by toothed belts rather than by chains (for the very first time in a Ferrari), and the engine was fed by two triple-choke downdraught Weber carburetors above each cylinder bank rather than by the

***Bottom** 1974 Ferrari 365 GTB/4 Berlinetta Boxer and **below** interior*

familiar battery of six twin-choke downdrauft units in the centre of the vee. Although it was a good engine, learning useful lessons from the racing Boxers, it wasn't a classic in the same league as the stunning Daytona V12, and with 344bhp it didn't have quite as much power or flexibility.

Equally surprising, the mainly steel-bodied Berlinetta Boxer, as it quickly came to be known, was very nearly as heavy as the "old-fashioned" Daytona. Still, it proved to be almost identically fast, and that meant very fast indeed, with a maximum of around 175mph and staggering acceleration virtually anywhere in the speed range. There was no escaping the fact, though, that the first of Ferrari's big mid-engined flagships had a very different character indeed from the last of the big front-engined ones, and the debate about which was better began with the very first road tests. The fact was, by the time he got to the Daytona, Ferrari knew all there was to know about front-engined supercars, and the 365 GTB/4 was the pinnacle of the breed. The 365 GTB/4/BB, on the other hand, was a starting point, and it would have been remarkable had it been totally right first time.

Clever as the mechanical packaging was, the Boxer was never as grand a grand tourer as the classic Daytona, but then neither was very much else. It didn't have as much passenger space, it didn't have as much luggage space, it didn't have the fine all-round visibility, and with the engine immediately behind your ears, it wasn't quiet. It had its plus points, though: with its lighter front end it had less muscle-testing steering, and in general it was a very friendly, uncomplicated, satisfying vehicle to drive. If it had one more problem it was what happened if

***Above** 1984 Ferrari Berlinetta Boxer 512i and **left** engine detail*

you overstepped the mark. Aggressive as it looked, and even with its very high limits, the Daytona was actually quite a forgiving car as it neared its limits. The Boxer looked milder and had virtually the same levels of grip and handling, but get it wrong at the outer limits and it took a lot more sorting out. That, of course, was the other penalty of the mid-engined layout for the "ordinary" driver, as opposed to the Grand Prix star. Let's just say that for every tester who loved it, there was one who didn't.

Fortunately for Ferrari, enough people did like it to claw back most of the ground Ferrari had lost to Lamborghini's supercar superstars, which weren't immune from problems either. Although the BB didn't sell particularly quickly in its early years—fewer than 400 cars between 1973 and 1976—that was as much to do with world economies and oil shortages as anything else, and in general Ferrari could be satisfied with the way his first full-sized mid-engined model had been accepted.

He did not let things stand still for very long. In 1976, the flat-12's capacity was increased to five liters, taking power up to 360bhp and performance up by just a click or two more while meeting new emissions regulations, which once again was actually a more important target than adding power. What's more, the second-generation —using Ferrari's other type designation as the 512 BB, for five liters, twelve cylinders and Berlinetta Boxer—was made more reliable, with dry-pan lubrication and an improved clutch. It was also less tiring at high speeds thanks to revised gearing which, with the lower-revving big-capacity engine, made it a less frantic cruiser than before while keeping the colossal mid-range flexibility.

The looks changed a little, too, with broader arches to cover a new generation of wider tyres, a deeper nose to keep the front more firmly on the ground at very high speeds, and some small cooling ducts for the hard-worked rear brakes. The character changed quite a lot, and mainly for the better for most Boxer owners, as the design became more refined, easier to drive, and more environmentally friendly (well, as friendly as a 360bhp 5-liter flat-12 could be) without losing anything in terms of performance.

Regulations tighten, standards rise

The environmental issue was the trigger for the next round of changes to the Boxer too, in 1981, when the 512 BB gained Bosch fuel injection to become the 512 BBi. That cost it around 20bhp but meant Ferrari could still sell it for a few more years—until 1984, in fact, when Ferrari's first mid-engined generation gave way to the second.

More accurately, these changes meant that Ferrari could still sell it for a few more years in Europe; they couldn't sell the BBi, even with its emissions-reducing improvements, in America, and that was a big problem. The market for hugely expensive supercars was always a tough battleground, and not being able to sell in America made it even more difficult to survive. More than any other factor, that was what pushed Ferrari into replacing the Boxer when he did.

As so often, it was a move Enzo Ferrari stubbornly resisted, and for as long as he could. He had known for long enough that the problem existed. With a growing pollution problem and increasing public pressure to do something about it, American federal laws had already started to be sensitive about emissions by the time the original Boxer was launched in the early 1970s. And they would only get tougher. It came to be so bad that even industry people made jokes about it. "How do you check whether all the smog equipment has been fitted on the latest model? You lift the hood and pour in a bucket of water. If any comes out underneath, something's missing."

America was growing ever harder on crash performance, too, and in a time before airbags this was the age of big bumpers and lots of body armour. Neither of these things suited Ferrari's style. He didn't build wonderfully exotic, race-bred engines only to see them strangled by emissions equipment he wouldn't have thought necessary anyway, and he didn't build beautiful cars to see them made ugly by huge rubber bumpers. So for a while he went through the motions, but when he thought there was more to be lost than gained he simply turned his back.

For a while it was a luxury Enzo could afford. The twelve-cylinder models, though expensive, sold quite well in America, and profitably, but in the larger scheme of things the big Ferraris only sold in what the mainstream motor industry would think of as tiny numbers—the type of numbers, even without Ferrari's other objections, that could barely justify a huge investment in meeting federal rules that would probably change again anyway as soon as the work was finished.

Right *1984 Ferrari Berlinetta Boxer 512i showing the radiator and pop-up headlights*

Above 1984 Ferrari Berlinetta Boxer 512i showing the rather large liftable lids, no fun to handle in a wind

Although he could no longer sell the big V12s in the USA, he could still sell decent numbers of the smaller V8 models, and it was considerably easier to make those meet the regulations.

Unfortunately, even Ferrari couldn't bury his head in the sand for ever, because to a certain extent, where America led, Europe followed; never to the extent of the ludicrously oversized front and rear impact add-ons, but certainly with an eye to cleaning up the air and gradually making cars safer in accidents. That was why Ferrari had developed the Boxer in the way he had. The move from 4.4 to 5 liters in 1977 was as much to retain power in the face of reducing emissions as it was to increase it, and the change to fuel injection with the 512 BBi in 1981 was more of the same. But the fact was that none of that allowed Ferrari to sell Boxers in the USA.

Left to himself, he might just have carried on that way—he was certainly stubborn enough, and by the late 1970s he was already in his eighties—but on the production side he had Fiat to answer to. If Ferrari was prepared to ignore one of the world's biggest markets, Fiat wasn't.

All of which brought matters to a crunch. Ferrari (and Fiat) needed to be back in the USA, but the Boxer had been neglected for so long in American terms that there was really no way of making it acceptable even had they wanted to. Even if they could have pulled it off, the modified version would have been so far adrift of what it had originally been that it would probably have done Ferrari's reputation more harm than good. Putting even more pressure on Ferrari was the fact that while he'd turned his back on America, Lamborghini hadn't. If you wanted a Countach Stateside, you could still have one.

Rear engines require special cooling designs. ***Above top*** *The Lamborghini Countach had huge roof-mounted pods to collect air—this example is a 1989 Anniversary Edition, Chas. No 12681.* ***Above bottom*** *The 1973 Ferrari 312 B3 racecar had side-mounted radiators.* ***Above right*** *The 1984 Testarossa followed this example and had intakes which started in the door panels, and became a distinctive—if delicate—design feature.*

The answer had to be another completely new design, a continuation of something like the Boxer's character, but bringing the whole recipe up to date nevertheless and making it acceptable to rule makers worldwide. It also needed to have a subtly different personality to make it more attractive to a new generation of supercar customers, a generation that wanted supercar performance but not the rough edges, people who wanted a big Ferrari to be as practical and easy to live with as a big Mercedes—sportscar performance with executive manners.

That was the brief Ferrari gave to his own engineers and to Pininfarina around 1978, as the Boxer began to struggle. The new model would have to meet the appropriate regulations, it would have to be refined, comfortable, luxuriously equipped and user-friendly. It would even have to have reasonable luggage space, but most importantly it had to have Ferrari performance and Ferrari character. In a way, it would be updating the classic definition of the grand tourer.

Enter Testarossa

The new supercar did have dramatic new looks, one of its most striking features prompted by curing one of the Boxer's most basic shortcomings.

The Boxer's cabin could be a very difficult place to be. To push some weight forwards and improve the distribution, Ferrari had put the Boxer's huge radiator in the front, with the hot water pipes running back past the cabin to the mid-mounted engine. Without resorting to power-sapping air-conditioning, a Boxer cabin could be a very hot place during travel. That wouldn't be acceptable in the new model, with its emphasis on comfortable usability, so Ferrari needed a new layout. He turned to racing ideas, where it was now usual to have the radiators at

Left *1984 Ferrari Testarossa and* ***below bottom*** *interior*

Below top *The flat 12 Boxer engine of a 1986 Ferrari Testarossa, Chas. No 59981*

the sides of the car, just ahead of the rear wheels. By doing that on the road car Ferrari could solve the problem of roasting passengers, create more luggage space in the front and give an even better weight distribution, by getting a fairly heavy component into the middle rather t han hang it outside the axle lines. That would reduce the "dumb-bell" effect and make the vehicle more forgiving around its limits, and it would be reasonably easy to find the space because the latest generation of tires meant the new car would have to have significantly wider rear bodywork anyway.

There was one problem, but it was mainly Pininfarina's: how to get big masses of air into the radiators without having to resort to the type of huge add-on air scoops the Countach had sported. Their solution turned out to be the defining styling feature of the automobile. They devised deep, curving side ducts running through the doors and into the rear flanks, split by five horizontal strakes. They became the obvious talking point of an otherwise super-smooth and actually quite understated design. They were controversial, naturally, but they were functional and they were necessary, because in some markets the rules said that air intakes as big as these had to have some sort of grille over them (probably to prevent the car swallowing small children whole), and the side bars qualified as a grille. Otherwise, what mainly distinguished the new shape was its wedgy profile, its broad rear flanks, and the massive rear deck flanked by "flying buttress" rear pillars like those launched on the first Dino.

It took a while to come fully to life, but the new design was introduced at the Paris Show in 1984. For once it had a name instead of a type number: Testarossa, a name Ferrari had previously used on some of his most successful prototype sports racers. The name translated as "red head" and had originally been coined for the first Testa Rossa (the four-cylinder racer from 1956) which had red crackle paint on its camshaft covers rather than the black Ferrari usually used. So did the new Testarossa road model.

It wasn't only the colour of the cam covers that had changed. The engine was broadly the same as the final 512 BBi's, but with a lot of detail changes. Capacity remained at five liters and the all-alloy four-cam flat-12 basics were the same, but to help it meet all the latest regulations it now had four-valve cylinder heads, more sophisticated electro-mechanical fuel injection, and the latest generation of electronic ignition. Power was up to 390bhp, 50bhp more than the BBi had slipped to. It was also usefully lighter, which helped the handling as well as performance, because the engine still sat above the transmission and had its effect on the center of gravity.

Top *In January 1992, Ferrari launched an "improved" Testarossa, the Ferrari 512 TR. Engine development saw the power increased to 428bhp, with suspension to match and* ***above*** *updated interior*

Opposite page, bottom *At the Paris Salon in 1994 the Ferrari F512 M was announced, with power up to 440bhp, and the pop-up headlights replaced with fixed lenses*

Like the engine, the Testarossa's chassis was a developed version of the BBi layout, and brilliantly effective. It used a mixture of tubular frame and sheet-steel "unibody" center section and it was both longer and wider than the BB, which made it look a lot more aggressive and a lot more modern. Suspension was double wishbones and coil springs all round, and brakes were all ventilated disks, which in the early to mid-1980s was a typical Grand Prix racing layout too.

Good as the Testarossa was, it was no uncompromising racecar. It was exactly what Ferrari had ordered: a staggeringly fast grand tourer that was saleable in pretty well any market worldwide. It put Ferrari right back at the top of the performance tree. A maximum speed of around 180mph, plus sub-six-second 0–60 abilities, made the Testarossa one of the fastest true production automobiles in the world, but every bit as important as the headline performance was the Testarossa's changed personality.

You still wouldn't want to take silly liberties with all that power and weight hanging out behind you, but the latest generation of wider tires gave the Testarossa even higher levels of grip than the BB, and being longer, wider, lower, and slightly softer, it was a bit more forgiving than the Boxer, and considerably more civilized, comfortable, and luxurious. The brakes were bigger, too, and gave a lot more stopping power through the grippier tires. The redesigned clutch had a lighter action, the steering column was adjustable, seat adjustment was now powered. As well as no longer being a sauna, the beautifully leather-trimmed cabin had more room, more luggage space, and more equipment, including standard air-conditioning. So the glorious Testarossa had genuinely taken the Ferrari range into a new dimension: performance with luxury, practicality, and, most important of all, an environmentally improved conscience.

It deserved to be a big success, and it was. Between 1984 and 1992 the first generation sold 7,177 units—by far the biggest production figure for any "full-sized" Ferrari, and more than three times what three generations of Boxer had sold. And there was more to come when the Testarossa was updated in 1992 to keep it alive for a few more years, up to 1994. In fact, "updated" hardly does the changes justice. The 512 TR was largely a new model.

The visible changes were subtle, because the last thing the Testarossa needed was a new look; the most obvious differences were just a gentle softening of the hard edges around the front and rear, and a new engine cover. There were much bigger changes under the skin. Behind the driver, without changing the capacity, a huge amount of engine development—including new cylinder heads, inlets, and exhausts, but especially the latest, state-of-the-art electronic injection and ignition management—had hoisted power by a more than useful 31bhp, to 421. The 512 TR had also shed around 100lbs It was, of course, quicker than ever, and by a big jump: top speed was up to 195mph, 0–60 ability down to just about 4.5 seconds. Incredibly, it also used less fuel and made fewer emissions. The clutch was improved again, the transmission was improved, the engine was dropped 25mm lower, the chassis was made stiffer, the suspension further tweaked, and the colossal brakes made even more effective thanks to cross drilling and even bigger disks inside new, bigger wheels carrying even more rubber. The steering was made quicker, too. Essentially, the whole car was upgraded. Even the cabin was refined, made neater and more comfortable. All of which created a vehicle that was better again to drive, with considerably more performance and another level altogether in terms of roadholding and handling.

And the Testarossa line still wasn't quite finished. In 1994, at the Paris Show, Ferrari took it one step further forward with the F512 M (the "M" stood for "*Modificato*," or "modified," and the 512 M was just that, a modified 512 TR). The revised nose had fixed headlights rather than the earlier pop-up type, the rectangular rear lights had been replaced by classic round ones, and there were new five-spoke wheels with curved rather than straight spokes. Two new air ducts on the nose improved the ventilation in the cabin, and it was clear that the modifications were meant to make this Ferrari even easier to live with. But it was also more powerful again, as tweaks inside the engine, including lightweight titanium conrods and a lighter crankshaft, hoisted the output to 432bhp. It was another masterpiece, but this time it really was the last of the Testarossa line.

Above *The superb cutaways of the Testarossa featured in the original Ferrari press pack*

F40

The Super Exotics

For Ferrari, GTO is a very special name tag indeed. Before 1984, in almost 40 years of production, Ferrari had used the designation only once, on what many people still think is the greatest Ferrari sportscar of them all, the 250 GTO of the early 1960s. As described in our racing chapters, that design was the ultimate development of the 250 GT family, and although it was quite usable on the road so long as you didn't want too many frills, it was really a racer. Which was where the GTO label came in. GTO stood for *"Gran Turismo Omologato,"* and the *"Omologato"* part referred to the racing homologation rules.

Interpreting the rules

In racing terms, "homologation" (a term still used today and most usually heard in the context of a limited-production "homologation special") is simply the set of rules that governs eligibility for a particular racing (or rallying) category. It covers everything, from mechanical specification to safety requirements and aerodynamic limitations, sometimes even the logos that have to be carried. In most cases where a competition class is based on a "production" car, it also defines how many must have been built in a specified period, designed to stop a manufacturer building one-off designs purely for motor sport, within specifications but regardless of cost.

That, at least, is the theory. But to someone like Enzo Ferrari (and, in fairness, not just to him), the real challenge of homologation has never been simply following the rules to the letter, rather "interpreting" them in the most imaginative way.

In 1962, beyond the 3-liter capacity rules and much else, the homologation rules governing the World Championship sportscar class at which the 250 GTO was aimed required a production run of at least 100 vehicles. Ferrari didn't build 100 GTOs, and probably couldn't have, given its complexity and expense. He built 39, arguing to the authorities that, according to how he read the regulations, the 250 GTO was simply a version of the 250 GT SWB, which was already homologated. Eventually the rule makers, who would have been less than happy to have had a World Championship sportscar fight without Ferrari involved, gave in. So in 1962 what was originally called the competition 250 GT Berlinetta gained its O for *Omologato*, and became the legendary 250 GTO.

Of course, it was a wildly different model from the 250 GT SWB—which, incidentally, had already bent the rules in evolving from the 250 GT Berlinettas. The chassis was more spaceframe than tubular ladder, the suspension was heavily modified, the engine was in full race tune, and, most significantly of all, the GTO had totally different and aerodynamically far superior bodywork, in several versions. By the end of the year it had won the first of its three successive World Championships, and for a while, legal or not, it was virtually unbeatable. In later years, partly because of its racing heritage and partly because it really was such a masterpiece, it also became one of the most valuable of all Ferraris, the best of them changing hands for several million dollars.

Until the 1980s, Ferrari never used the designation again. When it reappeared it wasn't used for effect, it was used correctly.

It re-emerged at the 1984 Geneva Motor Show, as the 288 GTO. Just as with the 250 GTO twenty years before, the O indicated that the car had been accepted for a World Championship competition category. The difference was that this time Ferrari had actually built (or would build) enough to satisfy the rules. In 1984, that meant a run of at least 200 identical

Previous page *1990 Ferrari F40 showing the impressed logo in the huge spoiler, and wind-up windows*

Below *The first use of the term 'GTO' by Ferrari was the 250 GTO. This example is a 1963 250 GTO, Chas. No 4293*

Above 1984 Ferrari 288 GTO, Chas. No 55729

"production" examples, to qualify for the new Group B GT category, which would apply to both racing and rallying. So far as the rule makers were concerned that was a big enough number to prevent a manufacturer from building too extreme or too expensive an automobile for the general public; so far as Ferrari was concerned (and Porsche, and others) it was a loophole, a big enough one to tempt him back into the top levels of sportscar competition after a gap of more than a decade.

He had walked away from sportscars, not for the first time but this time apparently finally, in 1973. Having won everything worth winning in Ferrari's glory days of the 1950s, 1960s and early 1970s, Enzo was ready to leave sportscars to Porsche and concentrate his resources on Grand Prix racing, where he hadn't won for a decade. As it happens, the sportscar regulations of the late 1970s and early 1980s, which concentrated on purpose-built prototypes, wouldn't really have suited Ferrari anyway, so he was happy to stay away. But the new Group B regulations opened the door to Ferrari again.

Group B was designed to shift the emphasis from prototypes to production-based models, hence the 200-off homologation rule. It would cover everything from the World Rally Championship to what was still the most important race on the sportscar calendar, the 24 Hours of Le Mans. Although Ferrari knew that even he couldn't build 200 pure competition vehicles, in the early 1980s, when the supercar market was booming on the back of the yuppie economy, he had a fair chance of selling good numbers of customer models. That meant they would have to

Spot the difference, ***above*** *1988 Ferrari 328 GTB and* ***right*** *1984 Ferrari 288 GTO*

be usable as road vehicles, as the rules intended. But once Enzo realized that anyone who would buy a machine like this would be more concerned about specification than price, he knew he could build a model far more exotic than the rule makers had envisaged.

That didn't mean that Ferrari could afford to start from a clean sheet of paper, he couldn't, but that was nothing new—even the 1960s GTO had been based on the "ordinary" 250 GT. The perfect base for a new GTO was the compact, mid-V8-engined 328. Not that the new design would have much in common with the 328 save for the basic layout and the looks, but it had to start somewhere.

The 288 GTO unveiled

It was showcased at the Geneva Show in March 1984, and carried the number 288 GTO. The "GTO" meant what it had always meant; the "288" meant 2.8 liters and eight cylinders. The 2.8 liters, multiplied by an equivalency formula of 1.4 for its turbochargers, put the 288 GTO just inside the official 4-liter limit for non-turbocharged entries, but offered Ferrari the possibility of hugely more power than a non-turbo engine, with no significant fuel economy penalties.

The 288 GTO, styled by Pininfarina in partnership with Ferrari's aerodynamics experts, looked like a 328 on steroids. The wheelbase had been stretched by about 4.5in and the front and rear tracks widened to give the design an incredibly tough stance. The stretched wheelbase also made room for a revised engine and transmission layout, quite different from that in the 328. In the road model the V8 was mounted transversely behind the cabin, with the transmission under the cylinder block; in the GTO the engine was turned through 90 degrees to sit longitudinally, and the transmission (a new five-speed transaxle with a limited-slip differential) was now behind the engine. That classic racing layout conferred a number of advantages, but principally it made both engine and transmission easier to work on in the vehicle—a big benefit during a race—and it lowered the center of gravity to the benefit of the handling.

This, however, was also a design which went right back to Enzo Ferrari's old philosophy, that there was nothing to beat a lot of power. And the 288 GTO did have a lot of power. When it was launched it was the most powerful engine Ferrari had ever offered in a road model, and it stayed that way until it was replaced by the F40. It was an engine designed for high revs and big high-end performance, with big bores and a short stroke. The big bores also made space for four attractively large valves in each combustion chamber, which was useful given how much fuel mixture would be forced through it. It used not one but two turbochargers, each with its own intercooler—quite small turbochargers for maximum response without the dreaded turbo-lag, but together big enough to blow up a storm. A single wastegate pop-off valve restricted the pressure at which both could blow. For the road versions it was set at a fairly modest level, but still enough to give the 288 GTO a nice round 400bhp. In full race trim, with the boost turned up, it could give more than 600bhp.

Compared to the 328, the 288 GTO had been on a tough diet, too. Where he could, Ferrari had replaced conventional materials with exotic lightweights like those he used in the Grand Prix designs. There were lighter parts inside the engine, and the body weight had been aggressively pared down. The main shell was now in glassfibre composite with aluminum-skinned doors. The hood and the big, louverd rear engine cover were in the super-light Kevlar composite, while the internal fire walls used a mixture of Kevlar, aluminum honeycomb and fire-resistant Nomex—a version of the material originally used in flameproof driving overalls. Even for a roadgoing 288 GTO, which was actually a well-equipped and comfortable automobile, that had saved around 300lb over the weight of the smaller 328.

Below *Marvellously muscular 1984 Ferrari 288 GTO*

Add the two improvements together, more power and less weight, and the GTO had one of the highest power-to-weight ratios of any vehicle on the road, at around 300bhp per ton. In racing trim it could be expected to give nearer 500bhp per ton, which was a massive figure for a production-based sportscar. Even as a road model, the 288 GTO was shatteringly fast—in fact, by far the fastest road model Ferrari had made at that time. Eight years before the 512 TR could come close to similar figures, the 288 could nudge 190mph, rocket to 60mph in well under five seconds, and to 100mph in barely a blink over ten seconds. In 1984 you would have had to go a very long way to find a production automobile that could get near those figures, but even more remarkable was that the GTO was so usable.

The cabin was fully trimmed, with leather seats and proper carpets. It had plenty of room and reasonable all-round visibility, and although the 288 was wider and longer than the 328, it was still reasonably compact by earlier standards. The 288's brakes were phenomenal, with ventilated disks more than a foot in diameter inside huge, 16in split-rim race-style wheels. The amount of rubber on the road, even in the production version, was as much (and as sticky) as Pirelli could offer in the early 1980s, so the 288 GTO had phenomenal amounts of grip for its day. The all-double-wishbone suspension had been tuned to squeeze the most from the new, wide, low-profile tires, but for the road it still had rubber bushing to keep noise, vibration and harshness to a reasonable minimum. On the racers, of course, where comfort and refinement came a distant second to absolute control, the suspension bushes were solid and the spring and shockabsorber rates were a lot stiffer, and the tires wider. As a road model, though, nothing would catch a well-driven 288 GTO.

On the track, sadly, Ferrari barely had the opportunity to find out just how well the GTO would have stood up to the best rivals like Porsche and Lancia could throw at it. Ferrari built more than enough examples of the 288 to satisfy the homologation requirements without any fiddling: 269 between 1984 and 1985, including one for former Ferrari world champion Niki Lauda. But by the time Ferrari could have been ready to race, circumstances had changed. On the racetrack the GTO's biggest rival would probably have been Porsche's hugely powerful and technically sophisticated 911 clone, the four-wheel drive 959, but the motor sporting world was denied the chance of seeing this heavyweight prizefight. On the circuits, Group B was slow to get started. In rallying (where Audi, Austin-Rover with the Metro 6R4, Citroën, Ford, Lancia, and Peugeot had all created monsters) it had created machines that were simply too powerful, fast, and dangerous for the forest and mountain stages. In 1986, after a series of horrific rallying accidents and some high-profile fatalities, the sport's governing body outlawed the cars. Any chance of the 288 GTO leading a racing comeback was gone, and if Ferrari ever had any thoughts of building more, they went with it.

What the 288 GTO had proved, though, was that if a design was exciting and exclusive enough, the price tag was almost immaterial. The only way now was up. In 1987, Ferrari would have something to celebrate, 40 years as a manufacturer under his own name, and he planned to celebrate with his greatest road automobile so far.

Above *In 1988 Porsche produced the 4-wheel-drive 959 supercar*

Opposite page *The interior and the twin turbocharged engine of the 1984 Ferrari 288 GTO, clearly showing the longitudinal layout*

Targetting the Porsche 959

The new model had to outperform the 288 GTO, obviously, but it also had to outperform Porsche's new flagship supercar, their own spin on the old Group B regulations, the ultra-high-tech 959.

In 1985, the 959 had changed the supercar limits again. Designed within the same framework as the 288 GTO, the 959 in road trim had a 2.8-liter flat-six with four cams, four valves per cylinder, two turbochargers, and around 450bhp—more even than the Ferrari. It also had a hugely sophisticated transmission system for its day, with a six-speed unit and full-time four-wheel drive with automatically variable torque split, to find whatever grip there was at each wheel, no matter how slippery the conditions. The 959 also had ABS brakes (something the 288 never had) and computer-controlled suspension, with variable ride height and variable shocks. The 959 also had colossal performance, even by 288 GTO standards.

There were two road trims, Comfort and Sport. Comfort had niceties like leather upholstery, air-conditioning, a top-of-the-range stereo system; Sport was a bit simpler, but still far from spartan. Their top speeds were a couple of mph either side of 200, just under for the Comfort, just over for the Sport. And with all that power backed up by so much traction, a roadgoing 959 could get to 60mph in considerably less than four seconds, and to 100mph in just over eight seconds. It was by far the quickest road vehicle ever offered, the first ever genuine 200mph production automobile—yet, amazingly, it was just as practical and as easy to live with as any 911. If he was to celebrate his anniversary properly, this was what Enzo had to beat.

The car he created to do that was right on a par with the 959 for performance, but totally different in character, and the best news of all was that it was every inch a Ferrari from the classic mould. It didn't have any of the driveline complexity of the four-wheel-drive Porsche, it just had mountains of power and a thoroughly developed, race-bred chassis layout. It would be the last design Enzo Ferrari himself (already into his ninetieth year) would launch, and to recognize four decades of Ferrari it would be labelled the F40.

Ferrari didn't unveil it at a motor show, but he did unveil it in person, at the Maranello factory in July 1987 to a small and select group of journalists and personalities—or potential customers. In his own words, he was unveiling "the best Ferrari ever".

The F40 could stake a fair claim as living up to that description. At the time it was certainly

Below *1991 Ferrari F40. By now it had adjustable suspension, and a light on the dash to warn you to stop if the catalytic converters got too hot . . .*

Above *F40 engine design*

Left *The engine bay of the 1991 Ferrari F40 where you can just see the tubes coming out of the top of the shock absorbers, by which the suspension was adjusted*

the fastest Ferrari ever, comfortably eclipsing both the 288 GTO and the more recent 512 TR. In fact, Ferrari introduced it as the fastest road automobile in the world, period. It could match the quickest 959's 201mph maximum speed and beat its headline acceleration times with a new 0–60mph record of 3.5 seconds, and 0–120mph in a jaw-dropping 11.5 seconds. But it wasn't just the F40's performance that finally stole back the crown from the 959, it was the Ferrari's unique, uncompromising focus.

As a road model, the 959, fast as it was, had been astonishingly luxurious and docile. The F40 was none of the above, it was much more of an animal, much more a thinly disguised racing machine. It had none of the Porsche's technical gadgetry, none of the clever four-wheel drive or variable suspension. It didn't even have anti-lock brakes, because Ferrari reckoned that that would take away the ultimate edge of driver control and involvement. Above all, the F40 was designed for drivers who enjoyed driving.

In engineering detail it was fantastically sophisticated and advanced, but in concept it was as simple as could be: a classic mid-engined, rear-drive supercar with the maximum power in the minimum weight and virtually nothing else to blur the experience. In that respect, it took the 288 GTO formula a step further, and of course the starting point for the F40 actually had been the 288 GTO.

Its engine was derived from the 288's but had moved on again. Capacity was up to three liters and the bores were even bigger while the stroke was even shorter, making it even more of a screamer. With a similar double intercooled twin-turbo layout and a state-of-the-art engine management system developed through Ferrari's Formula One expertise, power was up to 478bhp. That was another giant leap from the 288's 400, and better than the 959's headline-

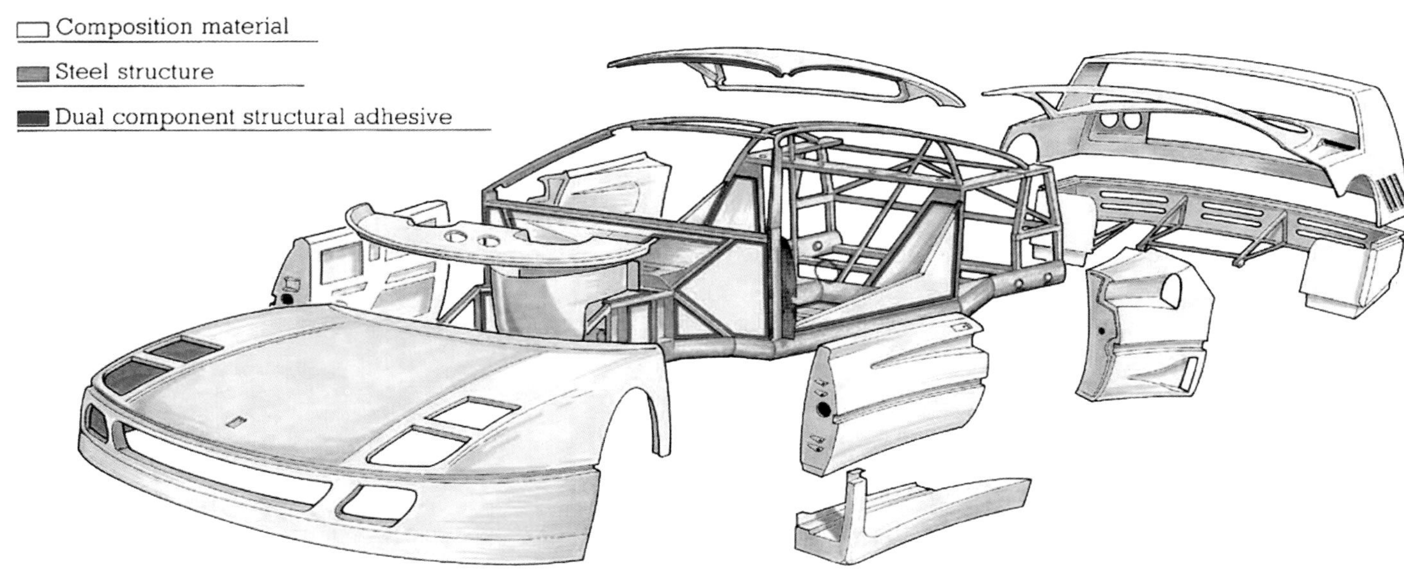

Top *With one of the first road cars to feature Kevlar, Ferrari was keen to show how it was saving weight and achieving enormous strength in the F40*

Above left *F40 shell in Ferrari factory body shop, 1990 and* ***right*** *F40 frames*

grabbing 450 of a couple of years before. And the F40 had been on another diet. The core of the chassis was again a welded steel spaceframe closely related to the 288's, but the earlier design's sheet-metal reinforcement panels and box sections had been largely replaced by composite materials such as Kevlar and carbon fiber, bonded into the frame in the same way as they were used in the Grand Prix Ferraris. It was a complicated, time-consuming and wildly expensive way of building an automobile, but the resulting chassis was around three times as rigid as a "conventional" one, and 20 percent lighter. The bodywork, too (by Pininfarina, naturally), had its weight pared to the bone. It was formed mainly in plastics and high-strength, low-weight

Above *The "office" of the 1991 F40, showing the supportive Kevlar seats*

Left *F40 production line, Maranello 1990*

composites, some of which, like the Kevlar in the high rocker-panel reinforcements and other areas of the cabin, were left bare. Unlike either the 959 or the 288, there was no pretense that the F40 was unduly civilized. The flimsy doors were simple shells which weighed just 3.3lb each. The cabin was bare except for a few splashes of grey cloth over the dashboard, center tunnel and around the roof pillars. There were no carpets, just rubber mats; no electric windows, just hinged panels through which you could pay your freeway tolls; no internally adjustable mirrors, no central locking—in fact, there weren't even any interior door handles, just cord door pulls like the original Mini. The F40 cabin was virtually as bare as any competition racer's. Even the seats underlined the race-bred character: high-backed racing-style buckets with holes for racing-style shoulder straps through lightly padded Kevlar shells simply covered with bright red velveteen cloth. The only seat adjustment was for reach, and the steering column didn't adjust at all. In fact, the only concession to convention was air-conditioning, and that was the simplest, lightest system possible, just to make the interior temperature bearable in front of that mighty twin-turbo V8.

All this brought weight down again, to barely 2,4420lb, and power-to-weight ratio up by another giant leap, to 410bhp per ton. That was what made the F40's performance not only so colossal but also so uncomplicated, so explosive. Fortunately, the machine had the chassis credentials necessary to handle it. A new generation of still wider, lower tires put hugely more rubber on the road, which contributed to improved stopping power as well as more cornering power. The brakes were bigger again. The disks (aluminum cores with iron surfaces to save weight) were cross-drilled as well as ventilated, and the calipers were four-piston racewear. The coil and wishbone suspension had adjustable shockabsorbers and carried enormous 17in alloy wheels in Ferrari's classic five-spoke racing pattern.

Above *Marcello Gandini's stunning Lamborghini Diablo*

Opposite page *1996 Ferrari F50. Ferrari's aim was to achieve the nearest thing possible to a road-going Formula One car*

When Ferrari said "the best Ferrari ever", he wasn't exaggerating, but, astonishingly, the F40 was still totally usable on the road—a road model with very little comfort and even less compromise, but a road model nonetheless. And how much you got out of it depended largely on how much you were capable of getting out of it. To drive it moderately quickly was deceptively easy; to find the borders of the envelope demanded both skill and a large dose of commitment. For the same reasons that there was no anti-lock braking, there was no steering assistance, and not much help either with brakes or clutch. At low speeds the F40's controls were fearfully heavy, the rearward visibility was laughable, and at any speed the noise and vibration inside were ridiculous, but take the F40 by the scruff of the neck and the experience was unrepeatable. The levels of grip, the precision and feedback of the steering, the power of the brakes, and the sheer violence of the acceleration were all on a level never before offered in a road design. It was the total lack of compromise that made the F40's character so unique, and so totally addictive.

From F40 to F50

Looking back, the F40 was a totally appropriate design to celebrate Ferrari's life and work, and it was the last major Ferrari Enzo saw, for he died at the age of 90 in July 1988. But he would undoubtedly have approved of the model that followed it too, the even wilder F50.

The stated aim of the F50, launched eight years after the F40, in 1995, was to create a road vehicle which allowed the owner to come as close as possible to experiencing a Formula One machine on the road. The F50 designation was to celebrate (a little early) 50 years of Ferrari production, and the latest Ferrari, like many of the first, was an open-top barchetta, although in this case a solid roof could be fitted to turn it into a berlinetta as and when the mood took you.

It was unveiled at the Geneva Show in March 1995 (although it would be a while before Ferrari started delivering the strictly limited edition of 349 cars), and it put even the mighty F40 in the shade. It was designed by Pininfarina, and was one of their more controversial shapes of recent years, moving away from the sharp lines and big flat surfaces of models like the F40 or the 512 TR and its final version, the F512 M, back to a rounder, more swoopy look. It was unique among outer-limits supercars in having the open-roof configuration, and its amazing lines had a lot more to do with aerodynamics than with just designing another pretty Ferrari face.

Aerodynamics is a science which becomes more and more important the faster you go, and the F50 went faster than virtually anything else on the road—though, oddly, it didn't go much faster than the F40, not that much faster than the latest version of Lamborghini's Diablo, and nowhere near as fast as the new outright supercar champion, the McLaren F1. What made the F50 different wasn't so much the numbers as the way it delivered them—its race car personality.

It went much deeper than just marketing claims. The F50 really did have a race-bred pedigree. It was based around a composite chassis using all the currently fashionable materials of the Formula One armory, especially carbon fiber, Kevlar, and Nomex. The bodywork was mostly of super-light carbon fiber, too. The F50's power came not from the previous-generation turbocharged V8 but from a big, non-turbocharged V12 that was a close relative of the Ferrari engine which had been a Grand Prix winner as recently as 1990. What it lacked in ultimate Formula One technology it made up for with a much bigger capacity than the 3.5-liter race engine, up to 4.7 liters in fact, and although it replaced the Grand Prix car's pneumatic valve control with

Bottom *1996 Ferrari F50 and* ***below*** *interior—more refined than the F40, but still very much a working space*

more conventional springs, and sacrificed the ultimate edge of Grand Prix tuning for driveability and long-term reliability, it was still a sensationally advanced engine. It still had five valves per cylinder, four overhead camshafts with very special profiles, and it still produced a monster punch of 520bhp. What's more, like the McLaren, it relied on capacity rather than turbocharging to produce colossal flexibility and instant, linear throttle response at any speed, without any hint of turbo lag and without any hint of the way turbochargers can soften the hard edge of the exhaust note. The F50's V12 was a real high-rev screamer. It was mounted longitudinally and drove through a six-speed transaxle which also incorporated a self-locking differential for maximum traction through the gigantic rear tires: 335/30ZR rubber on wide, five-spoke alloy wheels in an updated, curvier version of the traditional five-spoke Ferrari competition pattern.

There wasn't much else to come between the driver and that fabulous engine. No thoughts of four-wheel drive, no traction control, no four-wheel steering, not even feel-sapping servo-assist, let alone ABS—all of which Ferrari reckoned would make the driving experience less pure. More than anything, delivering the ultimate driving feel was the F50's mission.

With the detachable roof removed, the F50 is an open car but only just, as the windshield wraps around the front and the aerodynamic tail humps and roll bars snuggle up behind. The cabin is neatly trimmed but minimalist, the seats thinly padded, deep-sided, high-shouldered buckets that fit like a glove. Even more than the F40, the F50 makes little effort to disguise

Left *Rear, 1996 Ferrari F50 and* ***above*** *the engine bay*

what it's made of, and there are big, exposed flashes of carbon fiber and Kevlar everywhere.

The uncluttered, totally functional interior layout is the final clue to the F50's character. It is simply a very fast, very pure, very uncomplicated, ultimate driving machine. It starts with a racing-style button, and even as the big engine ticks over you can hear every ounce of the racing heritage. At low speeds it is docile, and even in the middle ranges it doesn't feel spectacular, but as the revs climb the power simply explodes. Amazingly, the F50 is not in the least bit temperamental, not even difficult to drive, until you begin to explore the outer limits. The controls are reasonably light, almost telepathically responsive. Even the six-speed stickshift in its classic open metal Ferrari gate is slick and quick. All these feelings of being one with the machine are what define the F50—what, in Ferrari's words, echo the racing experience.

It is, of course, staggeringly quick, with a maximum speed of 202mph and 0–60mph in 3.7 seconds, but those were no longer world-beating figures, and Ferrari didn't need them to be. It's the ultimate level of involvement which makes the F50 special. Its handling is razor sharp. There are no feel-killing rubber bushes in the suspension, which also features a Grand Prix layout, with pushrods and rockers between the wishbones and the coil springs. Yet with electronically variable suspension it gives a surprisingly friendly balance between comfort and control. The F50's light weight is as noticeable as its gigantic power, and it even feels compact.

Then, right at the edges of the envelope, it offers another level of ability, another degree of challenge only accessible to the truly skilled driver—again, exactly like a racecar, just as Ferrari promised. Which is why the F50 was exactly the right design to mark the 50 years, in a way by going right back to basics.

The Dino Heritage

If Enzo Ferrari had once been reluctant to start a family of compact, smaller-engined, "entry-level" Ferraris, then after he had entered into his manufacturing partnership with Fiat he turned out to be very good at continuing the line. He even accepted the idea of making the smaller models more and more a part of the mainstream Ferrari range. By the late 1970s these were no longer the poor relations, they were the core of the business, the part that kept the number-crunchers happy.

Once upon a time a good number of automobiles like these could have been sold on the strength of the emblem alone, but by the mid-1980s just being a Ferrari was no longer enough. Slightly perversely, many of the people who bought the biggest, most expensive Ferraris bought them whatever the price, sometimes for no better reason than to hide them away in air-conditioned lots while their value appreciated. Not every big Ferrari buyer was in that big-boys'-toys category of course, but certainly a proportion of them were. The people who bought into the V6 and, later, V8 family, on the other hand, were, on strength of numbers alone, a wider audience, and often more concerned simply with getting the best machine for their money.

They were well informed enough to know they had a choice. In this performance range, Porsche had long been Ferrari's most direct opposition, and Porsche could compete head-to-head with Ferrari on racing heritage and brilliant engineering as well as on price and performance—if not, in most people's eyes, on image. But there were other rivals in Ferrari's heartland. They ranged from the obvious ones like Lamborghini with the smaller Jalpa, Maserati with designs like the Merak and later the Biturbo, and even Mercedes with the SLs, to more obscure alternatives like De Tomaso, Lotus, and the even smaller specialists. Then, of course, for some people there was the totally different lifestyle option of a boat or a bigger home. All the time Ferrari had to fight for their custom.

Previous page *1988 Ferrari 328 GTB, from rear*

Below *1988 Ferrari 328 GTB from a more conventional angle*

***Left** Another stunning cutaway, this time the 328 engine. The transversely mounted 3.2-liter V8 now had four cams, 32 valves and produced 270bhp*

The 328 family

As Ferrari's "compact" designs went on, they grew in both size and reputation. After the progression from 206 to 246 to 308, the next step was 328, and that number made its debut at the Frankfurt Show in 1985. Following on from the initially controversial but ultimately very successful 308 family, it was the second generation of Ferrari's mid-engined V8 range—or the third, if you counted the *quattrovalvole* (qv) development of the 308s as a generation of its own. And just how successful the 308s had been is worth mentioning. In a lifespan of a dozen years the various members of the 308 family (including the Mondials) had sold around 17,500 units, and if you included the smaller "tax-break" 208s, that figure rose to some 19,000. That was more than half as many again as the total of all the vehicles Ferrari had built from the start of business in 1948 to the coming of the 308 GT/4 in 1973. By the end of the 308's run, the family accounted for almost half the Ferraris ever built.

So the importance of the next progression was obvious, and from the start the 328 family was a full range, offered in the usual GTB Berlinetta and GTS Spyder options, while simultaneously a 3.2 Mondial replaced the 3-liter Mondial qv and a 3.2 Mondial Cabriolet took the place of the Mondial Cabriolet qv. Following Ferrari convention, the new numbers revealed that the capacity of the four-cam, 32-valve V8 had grown again, this time to 3.2 litres. Power was up to 270bhp, meaning that the engine, as well as being bigger, developed a bit more power for each liter.

But you had to look pretty closely to see anything else that had changed. In fact, little else had, mainly because it hadn't needed to. The Pininfarina lines were unchanged except in a few details such as softening the sharpest edges, revising the light layout, and tidying below the rear bumper. Inside, the changes were again minor, confined to a bit more oddment stowage space and some revised switches and minor controls. Under the skin, too, the layout was as ever, with transverse engine location and five-speed manual transmission, plus disk brakes all round (though with a more effective parking brake layout), while in the Mondials, slightly narrower front tires made the steering lighter at low speeds without killing the feel through excess assistance.

Although the 328 wasn't hugely different, once again it was a better automobile—a bit quicker, but at the same time a bit nicer to live with. Top speed was now up to comfortably over 160mph, with 0–60mph down to well under six seconds, but maybe more significant was that peak torque had increased by an even bigger percentage than the power. That meant the 328 was more flexible, which made it more relaxing to drive gently, or in traffic. It also made it quicker overall in almost any real-road A to B dash, and for most, that was what kept its nose out in front of the chasing crowd.

More successors

By 1989, though, the chasing crowd was chasing harder than ever, and it was time for Ferrari to make a much bigger leap. In March 1989, at the Geneva Show, Ferrari showed a new version of the Mondial, the Mondial T. Then at the Frankfurt Show later in the year they launched an all-new successor to the 328, labeled the 348.

Just to look at the exterior of the Mondial T you probably wouldn't have thought much had changed, but you'd have been wrong. Save for the usual detail changes, the looks were more or less familiar, but what was underneath the skin wasn't. Since the 206 GT Dino, all Ferrari's mid-engined V6 and V8 models had used a transverse engine layout. Now, in both Mondial and the 348 Berlinetta and Spyder twins, the engine was turned to sit lengthwise, ahead of the five-speed transmission, which was still mounted transversely. That meant the engine could sit usefully lower in the chassis than in the old transverse-engined models, to the benefit of the handling. In addition, the chassis was now a fabricated unibody rather than the old-style Ferrari tubular frame, which made it easier to build, but more importantly made it stiffer and considerably more refined. So this wasn't just another upgrade, it was a giant leap forward.

This was the first Ferrari for the 1990s, and a pointer to future directions. It was a new machine for a new, increasingly sophisticated breed of customer, with a wider choice of rivals

Above *Cutaway of the 328 GTS*

Below *Final evolution of the Mondial, the 3.2 developed 270bhp, a 30bhp increase over the 3-liter QV*

Above left *1990 Ferrari 348 TB, an early left-hand-drive import to the UK*

Above right
top *1993 Ferrari 348 Spyder and* ***bottom*** *348 Spyder engine. The V8 was now increased to 3.4 litres, and output raised to 300bhp for the TB, while the GTS and Spyder found 320bhp at 7,200rpm*

than ever. Maximum speed in itself, as even Ferrari had admitted, was now only part of the package needed to sell a supercar. In the late 1980s Enzo Ferrari had said in a magazine interview that so long as the top speed was more than, say, 160mph, what was becoming more important was the performance up to that speed, the areas which made an automobile quick on any kind of road—in a word, acceleration, defined by headline numbers like the 0–60 and 0–100mph figures. Ferrari's stated aim was to continue to bring those figures tumbling, and by that yardstick the smaller Ferraris were now genuinely supercars, in any company.

The engine was another new version of the well-developed four-cam quattrovalvole V8, and as well as gaining high-end performance, with a new intake layout it had gained much improved flexibility. With capacity up to 3.4 litres and power to 300bhp, the maximum was around 165mph, and 60mph was reachable in around 5.5 seconds, but new looks also revealed a new character. For the first time since the Pininfarina 308 shape had made its debut more than a decade and a half earlier, the lines of the V8 Ferrari had changed totally, and the new design looked absolutely stunning. The body was a tiny bit shorter but the wheelbase was longer, so the overhangs were smaller. The 348 was superbly proportioned and neatly detailed. It was a lot wider too, on wider wheels and tires, so although the basic lines had been simplified and softened, the 328, with its Testarossa-style side ducts and dramatically square jawline, looked as muscular and purposeful as any of its earlier V8 cousins.

What was just as important so far as a new generation of Ferrari customer was concerned was that the 348 was also a more refined and usable vehicle. It even had ABS brakes, which was a first in the smaller Ferraris, but that was as far as the modern driver aids went; Ferrari certainly wasn't going to offer traction control or the like, even in a machine like this. With or without a roof, it was strictly a two-seater, but the additional width had translated into a useful amount of extra room inside, and that room was beautifully trimmed and fully equipped. The

Above 1995 Ferrari F355 Berlinetta

Below Ferrari F355 GTS

seats were a bit bigger and more generously padded, and of course they were covered in fine, soft leather. The pedals had a bit more space around them and weren't so awkwardly offset, which made for a nicer driving position. More than ever, the 348 was a Ferrari designed to be used every day.

There were signs inside, too, that both design and production had taken steps closer to the modern world. There were softer lines in the interior layout, especially in the dash and door trims, and an overall feel that would now look just as good in an executive limousine—a far cry from the simpler, more bits-and-pieces Ferrari styling of old. And although hugely increased production for the V8 family meant that even Ferrari now used the occasional Fiat parts-bin piece, aspects such as the super-clear instrument layout and the classic open shift gate left absolutely no doubt that, deep down, the 348 was still a Ferrari of the old school.

Into the 355s

In production until 1993, the 348 was another big success story, both commercially and in terms of continuing the Ferrari philosophy after the man himself had died. And it started another fresh progression, with the 355 family next up in the mid-engined V8 family tree.

The first version of that model was the F355 Berlinetta, unveiled in Geneva in March 1994, along with a targa-topped version, the F355 GTS. Styled by Pininfarina and built by Ferrari, the F355 had essentially the same profile and proportions as the 348 but the two were really quite different, the 355 instantly recognizable by its new side duct treatment, among other things.

Once again, it represented more than just another engine upgrade. With the 355, as well as the usual performance advances, Ferrari had set out to answer the main criticism of the 348: that for all its user-friendly credentials it could be less than friendly around its limits, when it could be more tail-happy than was comfortable for any but the most skillful driver. Now, there

Above The engine of the 1995 F355

was electronically controlled variable suspension and power-assisted steering, plus all-ventilated disk brakes. The variable suspension control was a big advance, letting the car ride as softly as possible for comfort when it was just cruising, but instantly stiffening when the car was driven harder, and there were standard and stiffer "sport" settings to define the overall feel. There was also a clever underbody shape to give neutral lift at high speeds, and bigger tire footprints gave colossal grip. Thus, the steering might not have been as razor sharp as the earlier model's, the overall feel not quite so precise, but the 355 was a lot more forgiving than a 348 if you overstepped the mark, and for most people that was progress.

Not everybody would agree with the new, less intimidating balance, of course, but what was unarguably a big step forward was the new version of the four-cam V8, which now became one of the finest engines in the world, period. Capacity had increased marginally, to within a fraction of 3.5 litres, but that was just the tip of the iceberg. The leap in power was way beyond the small hike in capacity. With the exception of the race-bred F50 V12, this engine produced the most power per liter of any in the Ferrari range. In fact, its 107.3bhp per liter also gave it the best power output for size of any non-turbocharged engine in the world, and that included the previous champion, the McLaren F1's mighty BMW V12, which had 103.4bhp per liter but was a strictly limited-edition affair with a price tag around seven times that of the latest Ferrari.

The secret lay in some of the most modern technology yet applied to a roadgoing Ferrari of

Above *1997 Ferrari F355 Spyder*

Right *Interior, 1997 Ferrari F355 F1 Berlinetta. When a road Ferrari has F1 in its name, it signifies it has "Formula One-type" gear shift paddles mounted behind the steering wheel, just visible in this picture*

any size. At a glance, it was little different from the usual 90-degree, four-cam V8. The big difference was indicated by the second "5" in the new number, because the F355's valve count had gone up from four per cylinder to five per cylinder—two big exhausts and three slightly smaller inlets which did wonders for getting the fuel mixture in and out even more quickly, and were also light enough to allow the short-stroke engine (which even had titanium conrods in the interest of light weight) to rev higher than any previous version. Add to that a brilliant new electronic management package that allowed individual control of each of the eight throttle butterflies, plus a sophisticated new tailpipe layout, and you had 375bhp on tap. That pushed maximum speed to a very impressive 183mph while bringing 0–60mph down to 4.7 seconds and 0–100mph to 10.7—and this in a car whose standard equipment now included not only ABS but also power steering, twin airbags, electric windows, and air-conditioning, all of them adding to the luxury grand tourer character.

There were other options to come. In Monaco in 1995, Ferrari unveiled a true convertible version of the F355, the Spyder, to sit alongside the Berlinetta and the targa-topped GTS. Not only was it stunningly beautiful, it also had a power-operated top and could be ordered with another new addition to the range: a "Formula One-style" clutchless sequential shift. That was still a manual "box," but it had a fully automated shift operated by small "paddles" on the steering wheel. All the driver had to do to change gear was flick one paddle for up, another for down, and technology did the rest. Again, it was race-bred thinking adding another driving dimension.

Left** The radical and mean look of the superb F360 Modena, with 400bhp available from its longitudinally mounted V8 engine, **above

***Below** Lots of horsepower*

The 360 Modena

To bring the compact Ferrari line right up to date, early in 1999, at the Geneva Show, Ferrari set new standards again with the 360 Modena. This time, there was no missing the fact that it was all new. The shape (another Ferrari by Pininfarina) was totally different, and absolutely stunning. The aim was to build a compact Ferrari that outperformed the already pretty sensational 355 in every area, yet at the same time took practicality and everyday comfort another step further. It would have more room for two people and their luggage, it would be easier to climb in to, easier to see out of, more usable again for the "ordinary" Ferrari driver; it would be a bit bigger to create space, and a good deal stronger to keep pace both with legislation and the handling abilities of the supercar opposition, but because power wasn't going to increase by nearly such a leap as it had from 348 to 355, it would be lighter. In short, it would have to be very special.

Right

top *An unusual view of the 360 Modena, unless you own one, and can admire it from your bedroom window*

bottom *The open road, and two 360 Modenas at play*

That meant another round of new thinking, another round of new engineering ideas. It started with a completely redesigned chassis structure. The 355 had moved on from tubular-frame to sheet-steel unibody; the 360 Modena moved up to a lightweight aluminum spaceframe. Its immense strength was as important for ever more demanding crash-test requirements as it was for performance, but there's no arguing that the stiffer the shell you can hang it on, the better any suspension system will work. The 360's suspension, like its chassis and its styling, was all new. Like the shell, it used mainly aluminum components, including the double wishbones and the hubs, to save weight where it counts most. Like the 355, it used electronic adaptive suspension, but this time its responses were even quicker, and overall chassis behavior had taken another leap. Super-clever aerodynamic detailing also helped the handling package.

Now, too, Ferrari finally bowed to some of the electronic safety nets other manufacturers had used for quite some time, so for the first time ever in a Ferrari there was a traction control system other than the one on the end of the driver's right leg. For the less skilled driver it was a useful safety feature, especially so when conditions were poor, or the road surface slippery. On the other hand, for the more adventuresome driver it was subtle enough to be reassuring rather than particularly intrusive or nannying, and depending on your levels of confidence and competence you could dial in more leeway with the sports setting (which also switched to a firmer, sports suspension setting)—or, of course, turn it off completely.

What made this different in a Ferrari from the way it might have been in, say, a big, powerful executive sedan was the way it was calibrated, to protect without taking away the balance or the fun. There was still scope to adjust the 360's line with power as well as through the steering, and still scope, on the right roads, to push the tail wide if that was something you felt comfortable with.

This was the nature of the 360 Modena, a design with many levels of ability for drivers with different levels of competence and enthusiasm. And underlying it all was another rung of power and performance, although this time, comparatively small increases in each. The five-valve V8 was stretched a tiny bit more, to 3.6 litres, as the number suggested, and power climbed to around 400bhp—retaining the V8's crown for world-leading power per liter. Maximum speed was little different from the 355's, at 185mph, while 0–60mph had been shaved another whisker to just under 4.5 seconds. Most impressive of all, though, was the relentless mid-range performance, matched by massively powerful brakes and steering which had put back all the sharpness and feel most people reckoned the 355 had lost.

Seamless power, massive performance right across the speed spectrum, colossal brakes and cornering power, razor-sharp feedback—it all added up to another level of ability again. And that, more than anything else, was what made the 360 Modena one of the greatest Ferraris so far. Not one thing, not even a couple, but the complete catalog, all working in harmony. The pinnacle of more than 50 years of Ferrari design philosophy.

Above *The 360 Modena has enough room for your golf clubs*

Left *Wide view of a 360 about to disappear into the night*

Back to the Front

Having apparently been so reluctant to slip into the world of the mid-engined supercar when others were leading the charge in the 1960s, in 1993 Ferrari dramatically turned the tables. At that year's Brussels Motor Show Ferrari introduced a new 2+2 coupé, the 456 GT. Twenty years on, the new range topper took up where the mighty Daytona had left off, with the engine in front of the driver. This, whatever some skeptics may have thought, was not a step backwards, more a giant leap forwards, and a headline-grabbing demonstration that Ferrari could still do things their own way.

The classic front-engined GT car

The 456 GT, which is still going strong in the early years of the twenty-first century, wasn't a masterpiece in spite of being front-engined, it was a masterpiece because of it. What on the surface appeared to be a revolutionary move was actually a reworking of the basics to create a supercar that combined the best of all worlds: the balance and performance of the mid-engined genre with the practicality, user-friendliness, and sophisticated style of the front-engined greats.

Leaving aside for a moment the question of where the engine sat, the 456 GT had all the mechanical credentials necessary to make up a 1990s supercar. That included a dozen cylinders (naturally), four overhead camshafts operating four valves per cylinder, big capacity, and big power—respectively, just under 5.5 litres and just over 440bhp. That gave levels of performance which we'll come to in a moment, but the brave move back to what had by now become an unfashionable layout created a car with a unique character. Lift up the rear lid and instead of a dozen intake trumpets you would find nothing more spectacular than a fully trimmed and quite generously sized trunk, which Ferrari equipped with a superb set of fitted leather cases as

Previous page *Ferrari 550 barchetta pininfarina*

Bottom *The Ferrari 456 GT, a classic whatever way you look at it*

Left and below The 456 GT not only looks wonderful but its front-engined layout gives it the balance of a true thoroughbred on the open road

standard 456 equipment. And where you might have expected to find the front end of the familiar V12, instead you would find two fairly roomy rear seats.

To understand what gave the 456 GT its go, you needed to walk around the front and peer under the massive one-piece composite molding of the long, low hood—where the action used to be, in fact, before mid-mounted engines became the supercar norm some three decades before, because the 456 GT, supercar or no, was conceived as a classically front-engined GT in the best sense of the name. Even by the mid-1990s, there were still other front-engined supercars in the world, notably from Aston Martin with cars like the ground-shaking V8-engined Vantage, and in a subtly different style from Bentley with their jaw-droppingly potent turbo V8-powered Continental R. But this was the first time in more than twenty years that Ferrari had put the prancing horses before the cart, so to speak, and they had done it in their most expensive, their most powerful, and their fastest production model.

It didn't just work, it worked brilliantly. The 456 GT, probably more than any big Ferrari since the 365 GTB/4 Daytona, offered everyday usability, reasonable accommodation for the Ferrari family owner, massive reserves of performance, plus such outstanding chassis balance that in terms of handling ability and agility it gave away little or nothing compared with its mid-engined rivals. In fact, far from sacrificing the edge, it brought back old ideas of character and individuality to an area which for too many years had actually been less innovative and practical than some designers and manufacturers would have had us believe.

So, whether Ferrari would have accepted the idea or not, the 456 really did introduce a Daytona for the 1990s and beyond. Like the Daytona, and like the vast majority of other Ferraris before it, it wore the Pininfarina emblem and oozed the classic Pininfarina feel. The basic proportions—the long front end, short tail, and wide, squat stance, as well as the strong roof and rear window lines—were unmistakably evocative of the last great front-engined Ferrari, the 365 GTB/4. Even when they were softened into such a subtly sculpted tail end, the big, round rear lights were an instantly recognizable recreation of a long-running Ferrari styling trademark. The hood ducts were pure Daytona, and the five-spoke alloy wheels were another

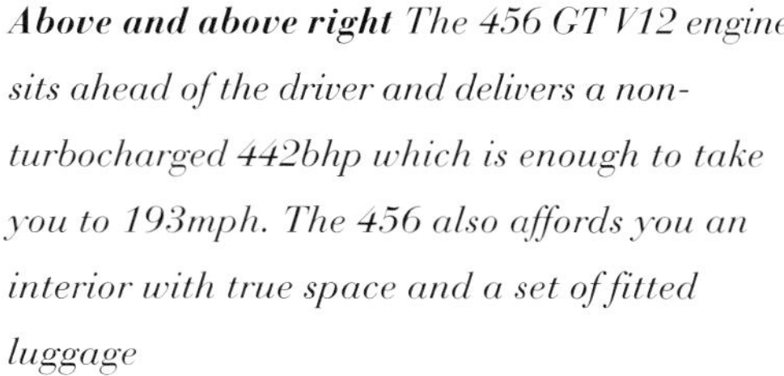
Above and above right *The 456 GT V12 engine sits ahead of the driver and delivers a non-turbocharged 442bhp which is enough to take you to 193mph. The 456 also affords you an interior with true space and a set of fitted luggage*

Ferrari styling signature. But the 456 wasn't a retro recreation of the Daytona, it was classic thinking brought right up to date by modern packaging and impeccably tasteful detailing, typified by the bold and functional side scoops, a strong Pininfarina theme turned around from front-engined to mid-engined needs.

Inside, too, you didn't need the yellow and black prancing horse in the middle of the three-spoked steering wheel or the crossed Ferrari and Pininfarina flags on the center console to know that this was a piece of pure Maranello magic. Dominated by the so-familiar polished ball of the spindly stick shift in its polished metal, seven-fingered open gate, the 456 GT's cabin had such a strong blend of character with functional simplicity that it couldn't have been anything but a Ferrari. Better still, it achieved that character without being outrageous or overstyled. It was exotic, but it wasn't intimidating.

In fact, it was easy to live with. There were mid-engined models with as much room for the two people in the front, but there weren't any with the 456's excellent all-round visibility, or its versatility. The doors were big and deep and they opened wide; the rocker panels were low, and as well as their backs tilting at the touch of a catch, the deeply shaped, leather-upholstered front seats slid forward electrically to allow easy access to the rear. There you'd find two well-shaped bucket seats which were perfectly adequate for even fairly large children, or two adults at a tighter pinch so long as they didn't need much headroom and the front passengers were prepared to sacrifice some of their own legroom. Comfort was standard now, too, with all-electric seat adjustment in every possible direction, front-seat heating for cold mornings, reach and rake adjustment for the steering column, and safety belts built into the front seats so that they always fell into the right place. Then there was air-conditioning, top-level in-car entertainment systems, power-assisted steering, ABS brakes, an all-new six-speed manual transmission with synchromesh on all gears, even a hydraulically assisted clutch action. All of which confirmed that, building on the driver-friendly characteristics of the later mid-engined models, this was a Ferrari to be used.

It was also a Ferrari with the performance and poise to match almost any of the mid-engined generation. The exceptionally light and compact 442bhp V12 was a thoroughbred, but in no way was it a temperamental one. Around town, or if you were feeling lazy, it was docile and tractable, but with the largest capacity of any production Ferrari at the time of launch, and the most power, performance was never going to be an issue. The 456 touched 193mph having passed 60mph in around five seconds, 100mph in just over 12.5 seconds, and 150mph in 25 seconds. Across that huge range it had the massive flexibility that only a big, non-turbocharged thoroughbred can deliver. In absolute straightline acceleration it wasn't quite a match for the smaller 355, but the depth of its abilities put it in a class of its own.

That extended, too, to its astonishing ride, handling and refinement package. While being far more exploitable for an "ordinary" driver than any similarly powered mid-engined Ferrari, the 456 GT had a balance that was virtually second to none. The basics were all-round double control arm and coil spring suspension, rack and pinion steering, and all-ventilated disk brakes, but the quality was in the detail. The 456 used an electronically controlled adaptive suspension system which continually monitored and adapted to road conditions and even driving style, whether gentle or aggressive. It offered three levels of stiffness—hard, medium, and soft—and a self-leveling system at the rear which allowed for the extra weight of either rear-seat passengers or additional luggage. The medium and soft settings offered real ride comfort on almost any kind of road, the firmest setting offered maximum control at maximum cornering speeds.

But what made the 456 so different from the mid-engined herd was that exceptional balance. With the engine set far back and the gears clustered in a rear-mounted transaxle, the 456's weight distribution was close to ideal, and with the near faultless feedback of beautifully weighted, ultra-quick steering plus hugely powerful and responsive brakes it had super-high limits with none of the hair-trigger nerves of the typical mid-engined supercar rival. In short, in going back to an "old-fashioned" layout, Ferrari moved the abilities of their flagship model to new heights.

Below *Ferrari 550 Maranello*

The 550 Maranello

Having re-established the front-engined layout's credentials, Ferrari soon showed that there was even more to come. In 1996, they launched an even more spectacular cousin for the 456, and this time the front engine didn't come as a surprise.

Ferrari described the new 550 Maranello as "Ferrari's interpretation of the twelve-cylinder berlinetta, with a front engine and a pronounced sports personality, for the twenty-first century." "The brief given to the technicians," they went on in their 550 introduction, "was particularly demanding: design and build a vehicle able to meet the needs of Ferrari customers looking for driving emotions and exciting performance, who do not want to forego drivability or comfort. Customers attracted by state-of-the-art technical proposals from a company which has always treated design as an esthetic solution to the demand for performance, and has always built its automobiles with sophisticated craftsmanship . . ."

The mission statement for the Maranello was clearly framed in those few sentences, especially in the part about "Ferrari customers looking for driving emotions and exciting performance, who do not want to forego drivability or comfort." The 550, to Ferrari, was another step in the evolution of the ultimate GT.

In a way, the Maranello's front-engined layout ought to have been even more surprising here than it had been in the 456, because this model really was the pinnacle of the range. It was more powerful yet more compact and lighter, it was even faster, and unlike the 456 it made no pretense at being anything other than a pure two-seater, albeit quite a luxurious one: where you might fit a couple of children in the rear of the 456, in the 550 you could only squeeze in a bit more luggage, maybe a golf bag, once the reasonably generous trunkwas full. The luxury was real enough: full leather, air-con treatment, twin airbags, electric seat adjustment, electric windows and mirrors, even such modern equipment standards as remote central locking and immobilizer. Also standard was that unique and totally recognizable Ferrari interior feel: the metal shift gate and metal-balled stick, the big, clear instruments and superb detail design, from the drilled metal pedals to the clever rotating air ducts.

With the front-engined 456 almost universally accepted as one of the finest handling of all 1990s supercars, no one had a problem in understanding the 550's "old-fashioned" mechanical layout. It was styled, again, by Pininfarina, but it looked very different from its front-engined cousin, or from any front-engined rival. It perhaps looked bigger than it was, because the lines were so muscular and aggressive. The only dimension bigger than the 456 was the 550's width, but its presence was huge. Again, with its long, low front end, steeply raked windshield, broad rear shoulders and chopped tail it looked seriously focused, and that sense of power was reinforced by the bold hood, front and side duct treatment and the low, wide stance.

Below *Pininfarina does it again, beauty and aggression*

Left *Ferrari 550 Maranello and* ***above*** *interior*

Like the 456 it was big on basic comfort and practicality, like the 456 it had a modern feel, and like the 456 it had an exceptional combination of power, performance, handling, and usability, only more so. The 456 was named for the capacity of one cylinder; the 550, following the other Ferrari numbering convention, was named for the total capacity. That meant that the capacity of the 550's four-cam, 48-valve V12 was exactly the same as in the 456, at just under 5.5 litres, but thanks mainly to a variable geometry inlet and tailpipe layout plus extensive use of lighter internal components (including titanium conrods) it could reach higher revs and produce more power and even more of that broad pulling power.

To put it in figures, the 550's all-alloy V12 had 485bhp compared to the 456's 442, and it was widely regarded as one of Ferrari's greatest ever road model engines. It gave the Maranello a claimed maximum of 199mph—tantalizingly close to the magic 200, but Ferrari didn't feel the need to exaggerate! It hit 60mph in 4.5 seconds, 100mph in 10.2 seconds, 150mph in 23.5, and kept on pulling hard all the way to the far side of three miles a minute. An even more impressive illustration of the 550's ability was the selection of middle-range performance figures, the ones that count on real roads, in real traffic. You could be lazy and let the flexibility do the work, or you could use the six-speed transmission to the full and sample its colossal punch. From 50mph to 70mph in third gear took just 2.3 seconds; from 80 to 100 in fourth took 2.8 seconds; from 30 to 70 only 3.9 seconds; while the spread of gears meant there was colossal performance across the range, to almost 50mph in first gear, exactly 70 in second, virtually 100 in third, 130 in fourth, more than 150 in fifth, then that quoted 199mph in the long-legged sixth.

Again as with the 456, all this was matched by the 550's outstanding chassis dynamics. With huge, race-bred, ventilated, and cross-drilled brake disks, four-pot brake calipers, and standard ABS anti-locking, it could shed speed even quicker than it could pile it on. It could go from 60mph to zero, for example, two seconds quicker than from 0–60, and with maximum pedal feel. The steering, too, was full of precision and faithful feedback. The power assist was subtle, and with only 2.2 turns from lock to lock it was quicker even than the 456's super-responsive set-up.

Below
top *The Ferrari 550 barchetta pininfarina is the ultimate "Little Boat" open roadster, if you aren't lucky enough to own the Rossa concept*
bottom *This is No 197 of the 448 barchettas built*

Then there was the 550's superb front-engine, rear-transaxle handling balance. The suspension layout was again double control arms, coil springs, and anti-roll bars all round, with electronically controlled variable shocks calibrated to give the perfect balance between comfort and impeccable control. It was attached to a hugely stiff shell, with an alloy body welded over a tubular alloy-steel frame further reinforced by an exotic steel-and-aluminum layered material known as Feran. It sat on a variation of the classic five-spoke magnesium-alloy wheel design, wrapped in sticky rubber 8.5in wide on each front corner and 10.5in wide on each rear. Add to that brilliant aerodynamic detailing, including race-style underbody "tunnels" which gave high-speed downforce without the need for flamboyant fenders and spoilers, and you had an exceptional dynamic package.

All this technology and tradition meant the 550 was a machine for all moods and all abilities. Depending on how you chose to drive it, it could be a pussycat or a tiger, but it was never less than brilliant, and like the 456 it had few of the mid-engined supercar's bad manners. It even had traction control as standard, but unlike the traditional take-it-or-leave-it system it offered three options: normal, sport, and off—the last only with the firmer suspension setting. It wasn't so much a necessity as a safety net, because the 550's handling was friendly enough to explore to very high levels. Ultimately it could deliver more than 1.1G of sideways cornering power, but right up to its limits it sent plenty of reliable information and was always ready to respond predictably to the right driver inputs. In other words, it was user-friendly, and if there was one way to sum up the modern Ferrari supercar, that could be it.

There was one more thing the 550 eventually offered that the mid-engined giants couldn't: an open-topped option in the 550 Barchetta, whose top retracted under a new and slightly clumsy-looking tail end with small headrest humps behind two tall roll hoops.

Latest developments

As ever, Ferrari does not stand still. 2002 saw the launch of a facelifted version of the 550—the 575 Maranello. Other than the Barchetta, this was the first significant change to the 550 since it was introduced in 1996—and saw some minor styling changes and some more major mechanical ones. Power from the 5.5 V12 was increased to a full 500bhp, the suspension was revised to improve handling still further, and for the first time the car was available with a version of Ferrari's automated-shift six-speed manual transmission, using steering-wheel-mounted paddles for clutchless up and down shifts.

The 575 carries the 550 to the next generation, which is expected in the near future, and that will bring more radical changes. A longer wheelbase, pushing the front axle ahead of the bulk of an all-new 6-liter V12, will give the new model a slightly more rear-biased weight distribution, keeping the forgiving handling but improving steering feel and improving traction. Formula One-style carbon fiber disk brakes are promised, too, and new looks. Then, after this, Ferrari should also replace the 456 GT.

That is the future for Ferrari, and Enzo would be proud of it. After all, when asked which was the car he was most proud of, he usually gave the same answer: "the one I will build next." He was often smiling when he said it, but he wasn't joking.

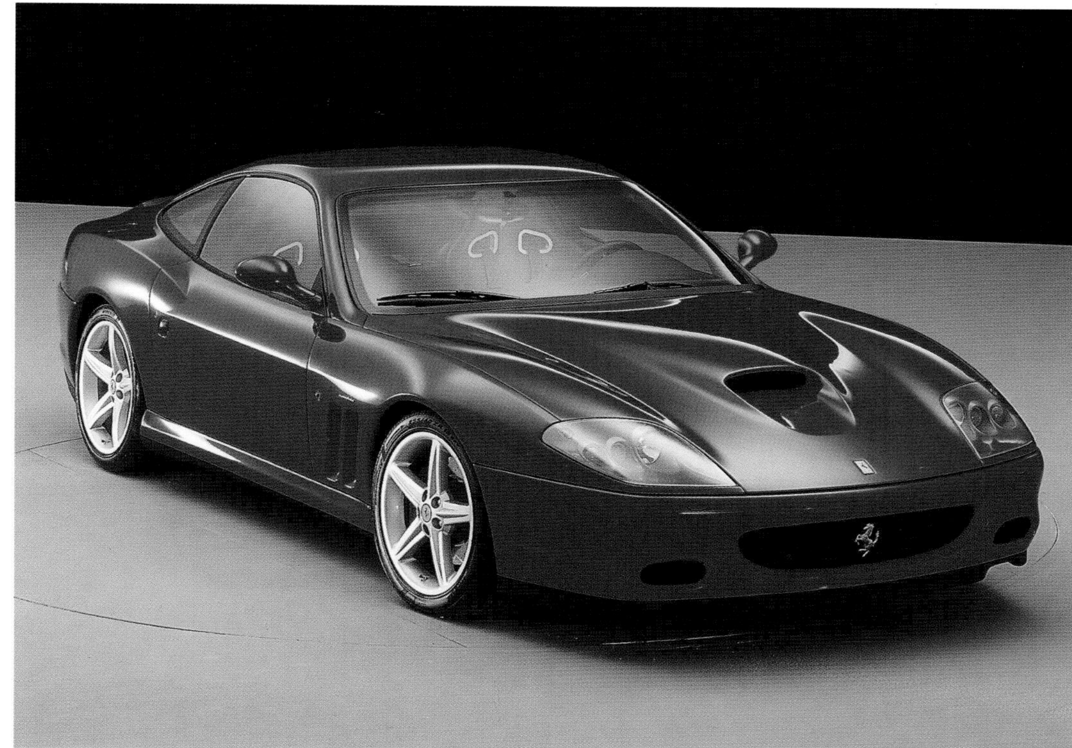

Left and below *Ferrari 575 Maranello*

Sportscar Racing Giants

For Enzo Ferrari, the British Grand Prix at Silverstone in 1951 marked an emotional peak in his life's achievements to that time. From the early 1920s, motor sport had dominated Ferrari's life, first as a young spectator, briefly as a driver. Later he became Alfa Romeo's team manager, later still founder of the Scuderia Ferrari, finally a manufacturer of racecars. But on that day in 1951, in only the second official season of Grand Prix racing for the Ferrari marque, the new competition designs from Maranello became world beaters.

Enzo Ferrari clearly saw this as the moment he at last emerged from the shadow of Alfa, the moment when Ferrari proved itself as a racing marque in its own right. As he wrote later, "my return to Modena . . . represented an attempt to prove to myself and to others that during the twenty years I was with Alfa Romeo not all my reputation was second-hand and gained by the efforts and skill of others. The time had come for me to see how far I could get by my own efforts. And the moment arrived and was consummated in July 1951, when Gonzalez, in the 4.5-liter Ferrari, for the first time beat the famous Alfa Romeo 159." For Enzo, finally beating his old bosses from Alfa Romeo was a defining moment. "When Gonzalez, at the wheel of a Ferrari, left the 159 and the whole Alfa team behind him for the first time in a direct confrontation with us," he wrote, "I cried for joy. But my tears of enthusiasm were tears of pain, too. Because on that day I thought, 'I have killed my mother.'"

The following year, 1952, Alberto Ascari won Ferrari's first Grand Prix World Championship (again beating the Alfas) and Enzo received a telegram of congratulations from Alfa's general manager. In reply, Ferrari wrote, "Dear friends at Alfa, allow me to begin thus this letter which I am writing to you after so many years. Your telegram today has brought a breath of spring air into my life. It has cleared from the sky every cloud, so that all I can see is fond past memories of you all. I lived with you for twenty years. How many events and how many men have passed by

Previous page *1963 Ferrari 250 GTO, Chas. No 4293. This car won the Spa 500km and came second at Le Mans in 1963*

Below *The British Grand Prix at Silverstone in 1951: Gonzalez raises his arm in triumph*

Left *Alberto Ascari at the wheel of a Ferrari 500, on his way to winning Ferrari's first Grand Prix World Championship, Silverstone 1952*

since then! Today I have remembered all and every one of them. You may be sure that, for your Alfa, I still feel the adolescent tenderness of first love, the immaculate affection for one's mother. Believe me . . ." From that moment, Ferrari's place in motor racing history was assured.

More than fifty years on, Ferrari is still easily the biggest name in motor sport. In the 54 years from the first ever race to the end of the 2001 Grand Prix season, Ferrari had contested more than 650 Grands Prix. Its tally of victories was approaching the 150 mark, and it had won nine Grand Prix Drivers' World Championships plus eleven Constructors' Championships since that title was added in 1958. Its sportscars had taken nine Le Mans wins, eight Mille Miglia wins, seven Targa Florio wins and another string of drivers' and manufacturers' championships. In other categories Ferraris had contested literally thousands of races, from the most ordinary of club races to CanAm, Formula Two, and the European Hillclimb Championships. Virtually the only great race Ferrari has never won is the Indianapolis 500, and that is probably only because it raced there just once as a works effort.

Through it all, Ferrari has been supported in good times and bad by the faithful "*tifosi*," of all nationalities. Come 2000 it had been 21 years since Ferrari had won a Grand Prix Drivers' world title, and there had even been years without a single race win, but for the fans the belief that Ferrari would bounce back had never wavered. The idea of Grand Prix racing without Ferrari was unthinkable, even to supporters of their bitterest rivals. Today, Ferrari remains the only marque that has been continuously involved in the modern Grand Prix World Championship since the day it began in 1950, and one of the few surviving teams which has always made its racing automobiles in their entirety, including engines and transmissions as well as chassis.

Through six decades, from the 1940s to the 1990s, Ferrari had been through triumphs and disasters, spectacular peaks and worryingly long troughs, but going into the twenty-first century Ferrari was back on top, holding both drivers' and constructors' world titles. And for fifty years and more Ferrari has always done it its own way.

Early wins

It began, of course, even before the first Ferrari car was built. In 1940 Enzo Ferrari had bent the rules, or at least worked his way around the terms of his Alfa severance agreement, when his Auto Avio Costruzione 815s appeared in that year's version of the Mille Miglia. Seven years later the real story began for Ferrari racecars proper in sportscar racing, and although Grand Prix racing naturally became the pinnacle of Ferrari's racing achievements, sportscar racing put down the marque's roots.

In May 1947 the first automobile ever to be badged as a Ferrari, the 1.5-liter V12-engined 125 Sport, appeared in a relatively minor race in Piacenza, in the north of Italy. Two were entered, but the machine due to be driven by Giuseppe Farina crashed in practice and could not start the race. The other was driven by Franco Cortese, who led the field until just two laps from the end when his fuel pump broke. Two weeks later Cortese scored the first win for the new marque, in another fairly minor sportscar race in Rome. Later in 1947, Cortese, Tazio Nuvolari, and Raymond Sommer added further wins. Ferrari was becoming the team to beat.

As described earlier, the designs were already starting to evolve, and those later wins in 1947 were taken by the short-lived 159, the first 1.9-liter stretch of the classic short-block V12 in a model that was otherwise very little changed. By 1948, capacity was up to a full two liters in t he brilliant 166, and Ferrari moved on from the lower levels and started to win the legendary sportscar races of the day. In 1948 Clemente Biondetti won both of Italy's classic road

***Right** This 1947/8 Ferrari Type 166 Spyder Corsa was first owned by Prince Igor Troubetskoy, and is believed to be chassis 01C, which was originally a type 125. It now carries Chas. No. 0101*

races, the Mille Miglia in an open 166 Sport and the Targa Florio in a 166 coupé. In 1949 he repeated both wins.

That year also saw Ferrari's first triumph in the greatest race of them all, Le Mans. It was the first running of the famous 24-Hour race after the war, and obviously Ferrari's first appearance there. The circuit had been extensively rebuilt after being bombed almost out of existence and Ferrari entered two 166 Barchettas—Italian sophistication against a field dominated by much larger but far less exotic French designs. In the early stages the 166 driven by Jean Lucas and Pierre-Louis Dreyfus (nicknamed "Ferret") led the chase over the two fastest French entries, until Dreyfus crashed as darkness approached. But by that time the second Ferrari, shared by Luigi Chinetti and Peter Mitchell-Thompson (better known as Lord Selsdon), had joined the battle, and during the night it took the lead. With Lord Selsdon falling ill, the driving became virtually a solo effort from Chinetti, who clung on to win by just one lap. At the end he had to be lifted from the machine, but the first of Ferrari's nine Le Mans wins was in the bag. More than any other event, this one race spread Ferrari's fame worldwide—not least to America.

That, too, was Chinetti's territory. The Milan-born racer had emigrated to America and he became the USA's first Ferrari importer, and one of the marque's most energetic promoters. It was through Chinetti that all-American sporting hero Briggs Cunningham became a Ferrari owner, and in 1949 it was Cunningham who scored Ferrari's first American win, in a sportscar race at Watkins Glen, New York, driving a 166 Spyder Corsa, the first Ferrari ever imported into the USA.

Above *The winning Ferrari 166 MM of Chinetti–Selsdon in the paddock at Le Mans 1949*

Below
left *1953 Ferrari 340 MM*
right *In the pits at Le Mans, 1954, attending to the engine of the Ferrari 375 MM driven by Walters and Fitch*

The victories grow

Although Ferrari moved into Grand Prix racing in 1948, with a supercharged version of the 166, and was there for the official beginning of the modern Grand Prix World Championship era in 1950, it was a long time before it turned its back on its sportscar roots—in an age when sportscar racing was second only to Formula One in its international importance. And the

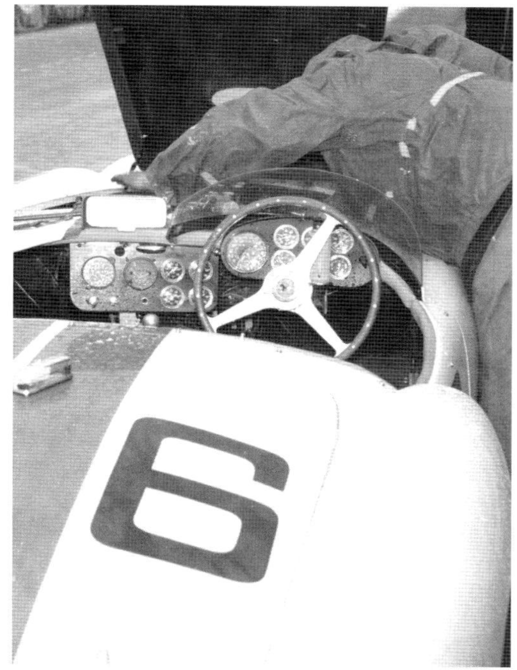

***Right** 1956 Ferrari 500 Testa Rossa*

***Bottom right** 1955 Ferrari Mondial 4S2*

success continued. It would be 1954 before Ferrari repeated its first-time Le Mans win, but in the meantime the list of major victories was impressive.

To add to Biondetti's Mille Miglia and Targa Florio wins (and his own Le Mans win), Chinetti won the Spa 24 Hour race in 1949, again with the wonderful 166, even as that model was growing towards the 195 and 212 developments. Gianni Marzotto won the 1950 Mille Miglia with what was officially listed as a 195S Berlinetta, while 1951 saw Chinetti and Pierro Taruffi win what was at that time surely the world's toughest road race, the Carrera Panamericana, with a 212 Inter. This spectacular and dangerous race covered almost 2,000 miles in mountainous country through Mexico to the US border. On public roads Chinetti and Taruffi averaged almost 90mph, covering the final leg at an incredible average of 114mph.

This showed that success in racing really did have commercial benefits. As we've seen, many of Ferrari's customer sales were set for a real racing career, while many of the others that were sold mainly for use on the road would also do a spot of racing on the side. It was the same for the big V12 models as well as the smaller ones. Ferrari's win in that second running of the Panamericana led directly to customer sportscars such as the 342 America Sport (which was largely intended for GT racing) and its more powerful derivatives the 340 Mille Miglia and 340 Mexico for the sportscar classes. Those, too, all had their roots in the works racing program.

***Left and above** the 1954 works Ferrari 750 Monza driven by Froilan Gonzalez and Mike Hawthorn*

By now, for Grand Prix racing Ferrari had switched his efforts from the small supercharged Colombo V12s to big unsupercharged Lampredi versions. In competition a parallel line of attack reflected that alternative engine philosophy. In 1951 Ferrari won the Mille Miglia, again on the debut of the 4-liter 340, which used the big Lampredi "Grand Prix" V12 rather than the smaller Colombo one, and which later evolved into the 4.5- and 4.9-liter 375 Mille Miglia and 375 Plus.

In 1953, the governing body of motor sport, the FIA, created an official international championship for sportscar manufacturers, and in its debut year Ferrari won the title. It won it again in 1954, and its victories that year included that second win at Le Mans.

Prancing horses for courses

Now, as well as the large and small V12 families (which grew through the 1950s with other sports racing models from the 1956 Mille Miglia-winning 290 to the 315—which repeated the win in 1957—to the 335), they had even more options as they introduced a line of sports racing models with in-line four- and six-cylinder engines, in both cases borrowing from a new generation of Ferrari Grand Prix engines. Through the early and mid-1950s, the four-pot Ferraris ranged from 2 liters in the 500 family (including Mondial and Testa Rossa versions) through the 2.5-liter 625 (with Targa Florio and Le Mans models) to 3 liters in the 750 Monza, and 3.4 liters in the rare 860 Monza. The Lampredi-designed sixes comprised the 3.7-liter and 4.4-liter 118 and 121 Le Mans, also known as the 376S and 446S respectively.

The object of the exercise was to have power to suit every kind of circuit and every kind of event, not just for the flat-out long-distance road races but also for the shorter, tighter circuits that were also part of the championship picture and where, in 1955, Ferrari was hard pushed, in particular, to keep up with Mercedes. As it turned out, the six-cylinder models didn't really

Right The smoking aftermath of the 1955 Le Mans disaster: the crash of Levegh's 300SLR Mercedes

Below 1958 Ferrari 250 Testa Rossa ex Squadra Largatixa, Brazil

achieve much and were quietly pushed aside after 1955, but the four-cylinder machines were far more numerous and a little more successful, the 860 Monza giving Ferrari a 1–2 finish at Sebring in 1955 and the 625 taking third overall and a prototype class win at Le Mans in 1956.

Putting all that into the shade was the success of one of the most famous Ferrari sports racers of them all, the 250 Testa Rossa series. The first 250 Testa Rossa arrived for the 1957 season as the sportscar championship rules, in the aftermath of the recent Le Mans disaster, were changed to limit capacity, and supposedly to control speeds and limit the dangers. It was both a works machine and a customer favorite, and it was a masterpiece. From the start, the Testa Rossa (named after its red-crackle-painted camshaft covers) was a winner whose tally eventually included victories in the Targa Florio, at Sebring, Le Mans and Buenos Aires.

The overall effect of this stable of prancing horses for specific courses was that Ferrari was now almost unbeatable in the manufacturers' division of world championship sportscar racing. In fact, between 1953 and 1961, the only manufacturers who did beat them to that championship were Mercedes Benz in 1955 and Aston Martin in 1959—respectively, against a background of tragedy, and through unexpectedly strong opposition.

Mercedes' year, 1955, saw motor sport's biggest disaster, when one of Mercedes' works 300SL cars crashed into the crowded start-line terraces at Le Mans, killing its driver, Pierre Levegh, and some 85 spectators. Some time after the accident the remaining Mercedes team entries were withdrawn from the race. Controversially, though, the Jaguars—which had been disputing the lead with the fastest of the Mercedes and the Ferraris at the time of the disaster—were not, even though Mike Hawthorn's D-type had played a central role in the accident, cutting across into the pits and causing Lance Macklin's Austin Healey to swerve in front of the much faster Levegh Mercedes, where its sloping tail became a launching ramp. Hawthorn, driving with Ivor Bueb, went on to win the race, but Mercedes dominated the rest of the season as the world wondered whether motor racing could continue at all.

After three more championship-winning years, Ferrari started the 1959 season with the latest versions of the 3-liter V12-engined 250 Testa Rossa, and won the first race, at Sebring,

with the four-driver combination of Phil Hill, Dan Gurney, Olivier Gendebien, and Chuck Daigh. But they failed to win another sportscar event all year, Aston taking the double of Le Mans and the championship.

In between those Mercedes and Aston Martin upsets, in 1958, Ferrari had won the big one, Le Mans, for the third time with Phil Hill and Olivier Gendebien in another 250 Testa Rossa. They went on to win it every year from 1960 to 1965, making Ferrari the 24-Hour race's most prolific winner until Porsche eventually overhauled that record when Ferrari turned their backs

Above
left *Mike Hawthorn at speed, Ferrari 250 Testa Rossa, Le Mans 1958*
right *The 1958 Le Mans-winning 250 Testa Rossa of Phil Hill and Olivier Gendebien*

Left *The 1960 Le Mans-winning 250 Testa Rossa of Phil Hill and Olivier Gendebien*

***Above** The Masten Gregory–Jochen Rindt Ferrari 275 LM driving to victory in the 1965 Le Mans*

on the race, and on sportscar racing of any kind. That was something Enzo Ferrari often did when it suited him, for practical or political purposes; but usually he came back when it suited him too, or when he felt he had made his point.

By the early 1960s, alongside the models described above, the 3-liter V12 250 family and its derivatives, from 250S to 250 GT to Tour de France to SWB to GTO, had enjoyed a full decade of success at the very highest level of GT racing. But now Ferrari faced his toughest challenge in many years on the sportscar front, and the confrontation changed the face of the sport for ever.

It could have changed the face of Ferrari even more dramatically. The new rival was one of the most powerful in the industry, the Ford Motor Company, and what the American giant lacked in experience it would eventually compensate for with a huge budget and unswerving determination. Before it started to reap the rewards, Ford's eyes turned to Ferrari—not as a rival, but as a potential way into the winners' circle without having to do it all itself. Ford's overall ambition was to promote the new, youthful sporting image that would make it the fastest-selling manufacturer in the world by the mid-1960s. The thinking was that it could win over the market by winning on the race track, and over the coming decade, under the banner of "Total Performance," its efforts would span everything from rallying to Grand Prix racing and Indianapolis. But to Ford, perhaps the most important single race of them all was the sportscar classic, Le Mans.

To win Le Mans, Ford knew it had to beat Ferrari—or, as they first saw it, to take over the

Above The Rindt–Gregory Ferrari 275 LM in the pits at Le Mans, 1965

Italian concern. In the early 1960s Ford put to Ferrari the possibility of a deal which would see Ford assuming control of the Maranello company and creating a family of Ford–Ferrari road models and Ferrari–Ford racecars which would, of course, include a Le Mans winner. Slightly surprisingly, perhaps, Enzo Ferrari was not entirely opposed to the possibility; he reportedly negotiated seriously and quite amicably. But in the end an offer of US$15 million and the promise of a continuing role in the racing program wasn't quite enough to make Enzo sign.

So, instead of joining Ford, Enzo was faced with the prospect of beating off their multi-million-dollar assault on sportscar racing in general and Le Mans in particular. For three glorious years he managed it, extending Ferrari's unbeaten run in the 24-Hour classic to six successive races, from Olivier Gendebien and Paul Frère's 1960 win with the 250 TR to Jochen Rindt and Masten Gregory's triumph in 1965, heading a 1–2–3 with the beautiful mid-engined 275 LM.

Away from Le Mans, Ferrari had continued his love–hate relationship with the sportscar racing scene, but it's fair to say that so long as he wasn't turning his back on the championships, he was usually at least threatening to win them. Spooling back a little, in 1957 the Mille Miglia had been run for the last time as the dangers and the growing number of fatalities finally became unacceptable, and Taruffi had won driving the 315. In 1958, Ferrari won four of the five rounds of the sportscar championship, including the Le Mans win. It had an incredibly strong driving squad which included Mike Hawthorn, Peter Collins, Phil Hill, Olivier Gendebien, Luigi Musso,

and Wolfgang von Trips, Grand Prix stars every one of them. And, of course, they had the legendary 250 Testa Rossa, one of the greatest racecars of all.

Ferrari's sportscar development continued to follow closely on the lessons of Grand Prix racing, first with the adoption of the V6 Dino-type engines, then, in the early 1960s, with a switch to the mid-engined layout. Those appeared in sports prototypes like the lovely V6 246 SP, the V8-engined 248 SP, and the big ones, the fabulous series of 250P, 275P, 330P, and 365P. Those were the machines that kept Ferrari at the top until the Ford effect overwhelmed them, and then there were those even more exotic mid- to late-1960s gems the P2s, P3s, and P4s which between them racked up occasional victories in the races that really counted.

Above *1961 Ferrari 250 SWB Lightweight, Chas. No 2689GT. This car was 3rd at Le Mans 1961*

Bending the rules

These were complicated times for Ferrari, though, not only because of the arrival of Ford and the growing threat of Porsche but also because of the rule makers at whom Enzo Ferrari had so often thumbed his nose. In the 1950s, through Ferrari's first decade as a manufacturer, the highest prize in sportscar racing was the FIA's International Championship for Makes, a series effectively based on the small number of classic endurance races, including Le Mans, the Mille Miglia, the

Below
top *1963 Ferrari 250 GTO, Chas. No 4293. This car won the Spa 500km and came second at Le Mans in 1963*
bottom *the interior with spaceframe construction visible*

Bottom right *1963 250 GTO on a street circuit*

Above *1966 Ferrari 206 SP Dino*

Left *In 1964, a Ferrari Dino 246 rounds a bend in the Targa Florio*

Targa Florio, and the like, and that was the title Ferrari had won seven times between 1950 and 1961, Mercedes and Aston denying him the clean sweep. But for most of that time the detailed format of the FIA's major sportscar championships had actually had very little stability, very little long-term continuity. Sometimes the most important category was the GT class, sometimes it was the so-called prototypes, until the rule makers took the only other option available to them and from 1962 to 1967 ran the two classes side by side, each with its own manufacturers' title. But whatever format was in favor at the time, the key to success depended closely on "interpretation" of the rules, and no one was better at that than Enzo Ferrari. Continuing his overall dominance of the sportscar scene, he won the prototype categories in 1962 and 1963 and each of the parallel GT championships from 1962 to 1964 with a variety of machines, starting with the classic 250 Testa Rossa then progressing through the stunning 250 GTO and the first of the mid-engined racing Dinos to the 250P, which had been introduced for the 1963 "sports prototype" category. In 1964, the prancing horse was beaten in the prototype championship by new arch rival Porsche, but Ferrari won another of the prototype-based titles in 1965, lost to Porsche again in 1966, then bounced back yet again in 1967, before finally being overwhelmed by the might of first Porsche and then Ford for the next few years, as the FIA once again introduced a single championship, the World Sportscar Manufacturers' Championship, in 1968.

In 1965, too, Ferrari, almost unthinkably, had lost the GT championship, and to the most unlikely of rivals, Carroll Shelby. In the 1950s the flamboyant Texan had been one of America's most successful drivers. In 1959, with Roy Salvadori, Shelby had won Le Mans for Aston Martin and helped them towards beating Ferrari in that year's championship. Around that time Shelby had also come close to driving for Ferrari in Grand Prix racing, but had had a major clash of personalities with the notoriously rude Enzo. Shelby had stormed out of the meeting telling

Ferrari that one day he would be back "to whup his ass." In 1965, in the GT championship, Shelby kept his promise.

In between, he had retired as a racing driver and become a constructor, creating the legendary Shelby Cobra. He was also closely involved in the Ford GT40 program which eventually ended Ferrari's winning run at Le Mans. But it was with his own Ford-powered GT contender, the Cobra-based Daytona coupé, that Shelby finally beat Ferrari fair and square.

Playing fair and square was not strictly speaking Ferrari's specialty at the time. The design Enzo had used to win the GT title in 1962, 1963, and 1964 was the legendary 250 GTO, and that had bent the rules about as much as it was possible. The GTO was supposedly no more than a development of the 250 GT SWB, but in reality it was virtually a whole new automobile, and an outright racer rather than a "production" GT, which was what the rules actually demanded. Nevertheless, it was the class of the field in its day, and for a long time there was little to touch it—until Shelby came along with his Daytona.

Like Ferrari, Shelby had adopted a liberal interpretation of the rules, having the Daytona accepted as no more than a coupé version of the Cobra, which had already been built in big enough numbers to qualify it as a production model. With a mixture of ample power from the same kind of Ford V8s used in the GT40s, plus a strong chassis and extremely effective aerodynamics, the Cobra Daytona finally had the GTO's measure. It might even have won the GT series in 1964, but with Shelby in sight of grabbing the title Ferrari managed to get the final round of the championship, at Monza, cancelled, leaving Shelby with too few races to gain the points he needed. In 1965, Ferrari actually withdrew from the championship in mid-season, which took a little of the gloss off Shelby's victory, but Ferrari obviously did it knowing that he was a beaten man.

It was all part of the wheeling and dealing that plagued the sportscar game at the time, but Ferrari's next shot at bending the rules was a bit too blatant even for this company. For the 1964 season he offered up the 250 LM for homologation. He had only built a handful, but he argued that in the same way as the 250 GTO was a development of the 250 GT SWB, the LM was a development of the GTO. He didn't seem unduly worried that the 250 LM was mid-engined and new almost to the last nut and bolt, or that all except the first prototype should strictly speaking have been labeled 275 LM, because they all had 3.3-liter engines. He even listed it as a roadgoing model. This time the rule makers didn't share his reasoning, so Ferrari was forced to run it not as a GT against Shelby's Daytonas but as a prototype against Ford's GT40s, and in that company it was outclassed.

But there was a final twist. In 1965, Jochen Rindt and Masten Gregory were entered at Le Mans in a "private" 275 LM run by Chinetti's North American Racing Team. They ran as a prototype against the hot favorites, the GT40s. They couldn't match the Ford's pace, but as the faster cars (including all the GT40s and all but one of Shelby's five Daytonas) failed, Rindt and Gregory cruised home to victory, leading a totally unexpected Ferrari 1–2–3 even though all the Ferrari works entries had retired. With a Ferrari win in the GT class too, it wasn't a bad day.

Above *1966 Ferrari 330 P3 at Le Mans, driven by Baghetti and Maglioli*

Opposite page
top *Ferrari 250 LM, Chas. No 6313. This ex-Ecurie Francorchamps car finished second in the 1965 Le Mans driven by Dumay and Gosselin*
middle *Ford GT40*
bottom *1965 Shelby Cobra Daytona coupé*

Above *1967 Ferrari 365 P2/3, Chas. No 0826. This car was campaigned by British team Maranello Concessionaires*

Right *1971 Ferrari 512 M at Nurburgring driven by Muller and Herzog*

However, that would be the last time Ferrari won the famous 24-Hour race, as first Ford, then Porsche, Matra, Mirage, and Renault began to dominate with a new generation of what were becoming more like two-seater Grand Prix designs than the traditional racing sportscar classes Ferrari had dominated for so long. Nevertheless, it took Porsche until 1984 to match Ferrari's record of nine Le Mans wins, and Ferrari is still second only to the German company's sixteen victories in Le Mans' overall roll of honor.

The magic fades

It has to be said, too, that one big reason for Ferrari not winning Le Mans in recent years—when it might have been feasible for it to do so—is that the team had eventually turned its back on the race completely, and to some extent turned its back on sportscar racing. The cars promised more than they delivered in 1969 and the early 1970s with the original 3-liter 312 P and 5-liter 512P prototypes, and by the mid-1970s the retreat was complete although, having been outgunned in the championships (since 1968 rejigged again as the World Sportscar Manufacturers' Championship) by Ford, Porsche, and the rest, they did have one more flurry.

In 1972, to the delight of real sportscar racing enthusiasts everywhere, Ferrari bounced back with one of its most spectacularly successful years ever. The model that did the trick was the second-generation 312 P prototype, a 3-liter spyder closely based on the latest Grand Prix design. Sadly, the 312 Ps were not entered at Le Mans in 1972 as Enzo Ferrari was embroiled in one of his recurring political disputes over the rules—albeit one probably triggered by the knowledge that of all the races on the calendar Le Mans was the one to which the automobiles were least suited. But the 312 Ps appeared in every other championship race that year and, with drivers of the caliber of Mario Andretti, Jacky Ickx, Helmut Marko, Arturo Merzario, Sandro Munari, Ronnie Peterson, Clay Regazzoni, Brian Redman, and Tim Schenken, won them all to take the championship by a huge margin.

It turned out to be Ferrari's last great sportscar championship year. In 1973, it was beaten both at Le Mans (despite disputing the lead until the last couple of hours) and in the prototype-based sportscar championship by French rival Matra, and at the end of the season Ferrari pulled out of sportscar racing yet again, this time apparently for good. In the past, Enzo had always come back once he had got his way over whatever rule change he was angling for, but this time he didn't. Grand Prix racing was taking up more and more time and resources, and sportscar racing at the very top level was becoming more competitive and, oddly, as the rules changed again, less attractive for a team like Ferrari. Rather than struggle to compete in both categories, Ferrari switched all his efforts into Formula One and left whatever Ferrari representation there would now be in the sportscar world to the private entrants. That also meant that Ferrari would largely be represented by racing versions of road models rather than purpose-built sports racers, and although many of them performed honorably, even taking occasional class wins, the days were gone when a Ferrari could dispute outright victories with the far more focused works teams and out-and-out racing machines of the likes of Porsche, Matra, Renault, and the rest.

Bottom *Ickx at Nurburgring, 1972 in Ferrari 312 PB*

Below *1971 312 PB exterior and cabin, this car ex Ickx and Regazzoni*

Above *1973 Le Mans, the NART team Migault–Chinetti Daytona powers past a Corvette*

Below *Andruet and Ballot-Lena's 512 BB at Le Mans, 1981*

The last outings

By 1974, Ferrari had genuinely walked away from the championship, although it did have the consolation of a GT class win at Le Mans with an unexpected fifth place overall from a privately entered Daytona. There was another fifth overall at Le Mans, and this time the IMSA GTX class win, for Andruet and Ballot-Lena's 512 BB in 1981—another unexpected result for a not particularly suitable automobile that was officially a private entry but which clearly had some behind-the-scenes factory support. From 1976, the championship was split again, to bring back prototype and GT categories, but Ferrari wasn't interested in either of them. Sportscar racing was now quite poorly supported and the few privately entered Ferrari GT challengers managed only minimal success against the hordes of all-conquering Porsches.

In the mid-1980s there was a brief flurry of excitement for the Ferrari faithful when Lancia came into world sportscar racing with a squad of prototypes powered by 3-liter turbocharged Ferrari V8 engines. They were fast enough to be a threat even at Le Mans, though never reliable enough to capitalize properly on their speed. Come 1986, the Le Mans grid was finally a completely Ferrari-free zone. Privately entered Ferrari-engined Lancias and a Ferrari-engined Spice prototype put in a couple of low-key appearances between 1989 and 1991, and private 348s showed occasionally, but none was particularly productive until a Spanish-entered 348 took a creditable eleventh overall at Le Mans in 1994. That year also saw a Le Mans outing for the F40 (in private hands, of course) as the rule makers encouraged this new breed of ultimate roadgoing supercar to give sportscar racing just a taste of the real-life roots which had once made it so attractive. But again, although the F40 was right on the pace during practice, its race-day involvement was short and sweet.

And then, in 1995, there was a magic moment for Ferrari sportscar enthusiasts when the marque bounced back into the winners' circle in one of the biggest races of all, the Sebring 12

Hour race. It was the first time Ferrari had won at Sebring since 1971, and the winning drivers were Fermin Velez, Eric van de Poele, and Andy Evans. The vehicle was Evans's privately entered 333 SP, the model Ferrari had at last created to contest the sports-prototype classes of the modern world championships. Launched in 1994 for the American IMSA WSC series, the V12-powered 333 SP spyder became a serious contender, on the very brink of becoming a regular winner, but the factory were still adamant that sportscar racing wasn't for them, and the best they would do was support the handful of private teams who ran the 333 SP on both sides of the Atlantic.

In spite of all kinds of pleas from the organizers, who would dearly have loved a works Ferrari back on the front row of the 24 Hour grid, that applied to Le Mans, too. Although the two F40 "Evoluziones" at Le Mans 1995 were works machines in all but name, it was left to the privately entered 333s to fly the Ferrari flag. In 1995, the single 333 SP—carrying race number 1, which had been one of the organizer's carrots to entice the factory back—was the race's first retirement, while the F40s were overwhelmed by the mighty McLaren F1 GTRs, one of which went on to win.

The 333s were exciting newcomers, though, and as well as being regular front runners in other races they put Ferrari back into the middle-order results at Le Mans. In 1996, two 333 SPs topped the time sheets in pre-qualifying and captured third place on the grid, although neither of them finished the race. They managed to survive for sixth overall in 1997 from second on the grid, and eighth in 1998, winning the prototype class with no fewer than four SPs entered, but the single entry in 1999 was an early retirement, and come 2000 the Ferrari name had disappeared again from the blue riband of sportscar racing.

When it comes to Ferrari, though, it would take a brave gambler, even now, to say the story was over.

Above *1998 Ferrari 333 SP*

Below *Ferrari F40 Evoluzione at Le Mans 1995*

kg/cm²
2 4 6 8 10
OLIO
S.A.C.M.A.-MILANO
veglia
70 75 80
0 5 10 15
GIRI x100

Global Pursuits

For more than 50 years, by far the most important racing classes for Ferrari have been Formula One and world championship sportscar racing. True, for almost 30 years Grand Prix racing has been the only game in town for the works team, but there were times when they spread their net much wider. Before it retreated into a world of total commitment to Formula One, to the exclusion of all else, Ferrari attacked everything from the European Hillclimb Championship to Indianapolis, from the CanAm series in America to Formula Two in Europe and the premier "winter-season" races in Australia and South America. And when things were going Ferrari's way, it was a force to be reckoned with in almost all of them.

In fact, Ferrari's first major titles, the 1952 and 1953 World Championships for Drivers (won by Alberto Ascari) and the same years' International Cups for Formula One Manufacturers, came in seasons when the championship Grands Prix were run to Formula Two regulations, at a time when the 2-liter formula was temporarily a more important category than Formula One (which then meant 4.5 liters unsupercharged or 1.5 supercharged, and which had its own, non-championship series of races). It's true, too, that Ferrari's success in those earliest days came partly because it covered all available angles, with the small-capacity Colombo V12s for the supercharged option, the big Lampredi V12s (and later a family of four-cylinder cars) for the unblown category, and a succession of unsupercharged versions for the Formula Two ranks.

Formula Two laurels

The Formula Two models were the first to confirm Ferrari's potential. In the 1950 Formula Two Championship, the works Ferrari team won all ten of the races that counted towards the title—the first ever clean sweep in this class.

In 1947, the coming of the new Formula Two had actually been the trigger for the first increases in capacity for the Ferrari V12: first, very briefly, through the 159, then to the full two liters of the classic 166 family. While the first 166 Spyder Corsas could be used for sportscar racing with their cycle wings in place, without them they could also double as Formula Two

Previous page *1952/3 Ferrari 500 F2*

Right *1949 Ferrari 166 F2, working on the engine in the pit at Reims*

Left *Villoresi at the wheel of the Ferrari 166 F2, 1949 Reims Petite Cylindrées*

entries—and they did, both for the Ferrari works team and for a small number of early customers. From the start, they also proved capable of winning. Raymond Sommer set Ferrari's Formula Two ball rolling with victory in the race in Florence in 1947, with the 166 prototype.

Those 166 Corsas were two-seaters, of course, and although the second seat was covered over for racing, they were naturally neither as light nor as compact as they might have been for what was really a single-seater formula. So in September 1948, for the Circuit of Florence, Enzo introduced the first purpose-built Formula Two single-seater, type numbered 166 F2 and closely related to the first Formula One single-seater, the 125 F1. Like all his other designs, it was a customer model as well as a works racecar, and another instant front runner.

It dominated the 1949 Formula Two season, winning all five races it contested, with three wins for Luigi Villoresi and one each for Alberto Ascari and Roberto Vallone. In the Bari Grand Prix the Formula Two Ferraris took the first five places, and they suffered only one non-finish the whole season. Then in 1950 came that championship clean sweep for the works entries, repeated in 1951 when they entered six and won six, before Ferrari withdrew to concentrate on his new Formula One design. In private hands, however, the Formula Two versions carried on winning for most of the rest of the season.

By then, the 166 F2 had a De Dion rear suspension, and towards the end of 1951, as Ferrari changed his mind about deserting Formula Two altogether, it gained a Formula Two cousin, the 2-liter four-cylinder 500 F2, with engine by Lampredi. It was conceived to be more effective than the high-revving V12s on tighter circuits, where flexibility was at least as important as outright power, and it proved to be exactly that.

It was almost as effective on the faster circuits, too, so for 1952 Ferrari left the 166 F2 to the private teams and ran the four-pot 500 F2 everywhere. With this model, plus a formidable driver line-up of 1950 world champion Giuseppe Farina, Piero Taruffi, Villoresi, and Ascari, Ferrari simply steamrollered the Formula Two-based Grands Prix series to win their first world championship. Taruffi won at Berne, Switzerland, and Ascari, who had missed the Swiss race because he was at Indianapolis, won the rest. The 500 F2s weren't quite unbeatable, but the only

This page *1952/3 Ferrari 500 F2, Chas. No 05, ex Ascari*

race they did lose all year was in the non-championship French "Grand Prix" series at Reims, where they were unexpectedly beaten by Jean Behra in the French Gordini.

There was a rumor that the Gordini had had a 2.5-liter engine, and that's probably what it would have taken to beat Enzo in his first Formula Two heyday. For 1953, although he ran a '553 F2 Squalo' model with bulbous side fuel tanks in one race, the same cars with few changes were good enough to win the championship for the second successive year, Ascari again taking the drivers' title, this time with wins in Argentina, Holland, Belgium, Great Britain, and Switzerland, while Farina won in Germany, and the young Briton Mike Hawthorn won in France.

Oval adventures

When the Grand Prix World Championship reverted to Formula One with the new 2.5-liter regulations in 1954, Ferrari's interest in Formula Two ended for a while. But during the time Ferrari had been dominating the European Grand Prix scene, he had also run single-seaters at Indianapolis. At the time, although it was run to quite different technical regulations, the Indianapolis 500 was nominally also a round of the Grand Prix World Championship; more significantly, it was by far the most important and prestigious race in America. And that, not entirely surprisingly, made it very interesting to Luigi Chinetti. So, in 1952, it was Ferrari's ever-enthusiastic American importer who suggested that Ferrari should do what few other European teams did and prepare an entry for the 500, for Chinetti to run with factory support. The outcome was not one machine but four: one for Chinetti and the works team, three to be run privately in Grant Piston Ring colors. It was a convenient way of recycling the 1951 Formula One designs, which were no longer of much use in Europe because of the new rules. A batch of 4.5-liter V12 375 F1 versions was duly and lightly modified to become 375 Indianapolis cars.

The three Grant Piston Ring machines, driven by Johnny Mauro, Howard Keck, and Jerry Grant, failed to qualify. Ascari, leaving the Swiss Grand Prix to Taruffi, drove the Chinetti entry and, having started at the back of the field following an unimpressive qualifying performance, clawed his way up to sixth place before the extemely high stresses of the high-speed oval caused a rear hub to collapse.

Left *Ferrari 375 special that had originally been built to run at Indianapolis, but had an extraordinary career. Shown here in its 1958 form at the Race of Two Worlds driven by Harry Schell*

Bottom left *The starting grid at the 1958 Race of Two Worlds or "Monzanapolis," clearly showing the European and American racecars lining up together*

Chinetti thought it was worth another try for 1953, and at first it seemed Ferrari agreed, because he set Lampredi to work designing a new engine. But though the supercharged 3-liter V12 was completed, it was never put into a chassis, as Ferrari decided that with a new Grand Prix formula approaching he had neither the time nor the resources to continue. The project was abandoned, and Ferrari never went back to Indy. It seems, though, that this was one of Enzo's greatest regrets, as many years later he said that not winning Indy was his biggest disappointment.

As it turned out, no one else ever returned to race at Indianapolis with a Ferrari. Luigi Chinetti intended to try again, and for 1954, again with factory support, he had another special built, this one with a 4.5-liter V12 and a side-tank body similar to that of the 553 Squalo Formula One design. It was at least completed, and several drivers tried it on the "Brickyard" oval, but none got as far as trying to qualify it for the race proper. It wasn't a complete failure, though, as it ran in various other American competitions, from the speed trials on Daytona Beach in 1954 to a couple of hillclimbs in 1955 where it won twice, driven by the man who would eventually return to "whup Ferrari's ass" in sportscar racing, Texan Carroll Shelby.

Its next appearance was back at Indy when Farina used it in 1956 to gain track time before a qualifying attempt. He wasn't planning to use the same machine in the race, intending to drive

Above 1958 Ferrari 296 MI (for Monza Indianapolis*) driven by Phil Hill*

another Ferrari Indy creation, the Bardahl Special. Backed by the Bardahl oil corporation—and initially, it seems, with the approval of Enzo Ferrari, until he lost interest again—that car was an interesting hybrid. In effect it was a traditional Indy "roadster" chassis, by top maker Kurtis, with a 4.4-liter in-line six-cylinder Ferrari sportscar engine, plus American Hilborn fuel injection. Even Farina, who had left Grand Prix racing after suffering dreadful injuries in one accident too many, couldn't qualify it, and it didn't appear again.

The design he had practiced with, Chinetti's 1954 V12-powered Squalo lookalike, did reappear, and its next outing was possibly the most interesting in its strange career. In 1957, in an attempt to show America that Europe could handle high-speed track racing too, and with a view to bringing the best Indy drivers head to head with the best of Europe's Grand Prix and sportscar drivers, the organizers at Monza proposed a race using their new high-banked concrete bowl, opened in 1955 to replace the original banked track which had been demolished in 1939. This steeply banked track promised to be even faster than the gently cambered Indianapolis oval, but this first "Race of Two Worlds" confrontation didn't add up to much.

That June, nine Indy drivers turned out, but the promised European Grand Prix teams, including Ferrari, one by one made their excuses and withdrew before the showdown. Only Jaguar, with three specially prepared versions of the Le Mans-winning D-Type entered by the Le Mans-winning Ecurie Ecosse team, were actually left to challenge the Americans and their specialized single-seaters. With no time to source special tires for such a specialized event, the Jaguars had to be limited to 150mph on the punishing bankings. Nonetheless, they gave the visitors a run for their money in the 500-mile race, which was split into three heats. Six of the American cars failed to finish, but the three surviving Indy drivers were uncatchable, even though the bumpy track was like nothing they'd raced on before. All three Jaguars did finish, however, for an honorable fourth, fifth, and sixth.

Undeterred by this first effort, the Monza organizers repeated the Race of Two Worlds in 1958, but this time it was rather better supported—and among the European challengers were Ferrari. One of the Ferraris for that year was a reworking of none other than the old 375 special, which had been built for Indy and already had that remarkable, if largely unsuccessful, roller-coaster career. Chinetti entered it for the extrovert American Harry Schell, a fine driver with a family background as deeply steeped in motor racing as Enzo Ferrari's who had raced both real Ferraris and Tony Vandervell's Ferrari-based Thinwall Special in the 1955 Grand Prix season. Now racing for BRM in Formula One, Schell had a tough time at Monza with the ageing "Indy" Ferrari, now with a 4.2-liter V12, which finally expired halfway through the second of the three 167-mile heats.

But that wasn't the whole Ferrari story at Monza in 1958. To Ferrari, this wasn't just an interesting race, it was a high-speed shop window, too. Alongside Chinetti's old stager, Ferrari ran something a bit more up to date, obviously with an eye to a customer sale or two to the Indy fraternity: two works single-seaters, labeled 412 MI (for "Monza Indianapolis") and 296 MI. The 4.1-liter four-cam V12-engined 412, based on an older and heavily modified 4.5-liter Formula One chassis with an engine from the latest championship-winning sportscars, was potentially an outright winner. The 296 was in effect a 246 F1 Dino chassis, similarly enhanced, with a 3-liter V6 sportscar engine.

The powerful 412 MI, in particular, was very impressive. Luigi Musso qualified it in pole position for the first heat with a three-lap average of almost 175mph—by far the fastest lap speed in any European race and some 40mph faster than average Indy speeds at the time. He led the

Left *Luigi Musso's very powerful 1958 Ferrari 412 MI in the paddock at Monza*

race, too, but plagued by fumes in the cabin, fearsome tire wear and wheel problems, the Ferrari ultimately gave way to the more specialized Indy track stars. Musso, though, along with the other two drivers, Hawthorn and Phil Hill, did complete the full 500-mile race distance and finished third overall on combined heat times. The 296 MI, with Hill as lead driver, didn't do quite as well. With far less power it couldn't hope to match the big machines on speed, but Ferrari's future world champion qualified it at around 161mph, only to retire with electrical problems in the first heat.

That proved to be the end of the road for the imaginative but troublesome Race of Two Worlds, and neither design ever ran as a single-seater again, although both formed the basis for customer sportscars, also numbered 412 MI and 296 MI.

The CanAm series

In 1966, a decade after Ferrari's final, frustrating involvement with Indianapolis and the non-qualification of the Bardahl Special, the team embarked on another American odyssey. This one was marginally more successful, although by Ferrari's standards it could hardly be called a triumph. It was a rather half-hearted attack on the CanAm series, prompted, again, by Chinetti.

CanAm, the Canadian American Challenge Cup, was devised by the Sports Car Club of America to link their headline race venues with those of the Canadian Automobile Sports Club and create a series of races on both sides of the border for some of the most spectacular racing cars in the world, the massively powerful "Group 7" two-seater sports racers. There was little or no restriction on engine size or specification in CanAm, and the classic American theory of "there's no substitute for cubic inches" held good. The typical CanAm car of the late 1960s therefore comprised a relatively sophisticated and lightweight open chassis (and advanced aerodynamics) with the biggest production-based American V8 that would fit. Capacities of seven liters and more and power outputs of 600bhp-plus weren't at all unusual, and towards the end of the series, in the early 1970s, the colossal race-bred, big-capacity, turbocharged flat-12s campaigned by Porsche were developing well over 1,000bhp.

***Above and right** 1969 Ferrari 246 F1 Tasman*

Ferrari's CanAm contenders were never remotely in that league, but were another interesting aside to the team's racing mainstream. The series had been launched in 1966, and was instantly dominated by the mighty orange McLarens, powered by big-block Chevrolet V8s. For a long time they were completely unbeatable, and in five years they lost only a fistful of races, but that didn't mean the CanAm wasn't both well supported and highly competitive. Which, sadly, made Ferrari's one-off efforts look rather half-hearted.

Chinetti, no doubt working on the basis that Ferrari technical sophistication could make up for McLaren muscle, started the ball rolling with a design based on the 4-liter 330P3/4 model recently made redundant by changes to the world championship sportscar rules. He ran it first towards the end of 1967, entered through his North American Racing Team, NART, and driven by long-time Ferrari sportscar and Grand Prix driver, the versatile Ludovico Scarfiotti. Although Chinetti's rebodied sports racer was far from competitive, it was enough to make Enzo look closer at the series.

For the very last races of the 1967 CanAm Ferrari produced two factory machines, again based on the 330P4 but with capacity increased marginally to almost 4.2 liters. They were driven by Ferrari Formula One and sportscar star New Zealander Chris Amon, and the Italian-based Englishman Jonathan Williams. They contested three races and were never on the McLaren pace (nobody was); their best results ran only from fifth to eighth places, with a number of retirements.

The following year proved to be even less productive. NART briefly ran, with Amon again, what should have been a better contender, based on one of the works P4 sportscars, but it was no more effective. Then the Ferrari factory team, having promised a full-scale attack, failed to appear until the very last race. To be fair, they did bring an all-new and much more ambitious model, the 6.2-liter 612 CanAm, but even Ferrari could hardly have expected it to work straight out of the box, and of course it didn't. Having started its one and only 1968 race from the middle of the grid, it was caught up in a multi-vehicle first-lap accident ahead of it and never completed a lap.

Still, the team didn't give up completely. In 1969, with a mildly developed version of the 612 they joined in from the third round, at the Watkins Glen circuit near New York, and Amon at last gave Ferrari a respectable result: third place behind two McLarens. Then, at Edmonton in Canada, he went one better and grabbed second, followed by another third in the next round. But that was the end of the promising run, and it was followed by a string of retirements. Even a new 6.9-liter version of the V12 for the last two races failed to fulfill the early promise, and Amon finished 1969 as he had finished 1968, as an early retirement. At the end of the season, Ferrari turned his back on the American adventure.

Above *246 F1 cabin*

Other ventures

It was a tough time for Ferrari in Formula One as well: between 1965 and 1969 the team scored only three Grand Prix wins, while in sportscar racing they had finally been overwhelmed by Ford and Porsche. But Ferrari did still have one category, albeit a fairly obscure one, where they were all but invincible, and that was in the European Hillclimb Championship.

This wasn't hillclimbing in the familiar British style of gentlemanly attacks on small stretches of country-estate lanes, this was the serious business of storming up Europe's most famous mountain passes—legendary challenges such as Mont Ventoux, the Grand St Bernard, Trento Bondone, and Cesana Sestriere—in very specialized machines. When Ferrari chose to challenge, they were pretty good at it. In 1962, all-rounder Scarfiotti won the championship, ending a run of four years' domination by Porsche, who took hillclimbing very seriously indeed. In 1965 Ferrari interrupted another Porsche run, again with Scarfiotti, who took four wins from five rounds with the beautiful little V6-powered Dino 206 SP. Four years later Peter Schetty became champion with seven wins out of seven, driving the 212E with a 2-liter flat-12 engine derived from the 1965 flat-12 Grand Prix model.

There had been other Ferrari outings, too, alongside the headline grabbers, notably in the popular "winter" series in South America and Australasia, and a bit closer to home in South Africa. For those races, including the Temporada series in South Africa and later the Tasman series in Australia and New Zealand, the regulations varied just as they did for formula racing worldwide, and generally didn't follow either Formula One or Two to the letter, but they were usually close enough to offer a new home for older single-seater designs, and Ferrari was usually very competitive in all of them. Between 1950 and 1968, they won around twenty races in the Temporada (Vittorio Brambilla dominated the series in 1968, when it was for Formula Two cars) and dozens elsewhere in the world. Following earlier entries in the Australian series, they introduced in the late 1960s a 2.4-liter V6 version of the Dino 166 F2 Formula Two design, taking Chris Amon to the 1969 championship and New Zealander Graeme Lawrence to the 1970 title after he had bought one of the machines from the works—still a regular option.

Both Tasman and Temporada efforts at the time reflected the fact that, in Europe, Ferrari had come back into Formula Two with an effort every bit as serious as the championship-winning programs of earlier times. It started with the coming of the "production-based" 1.6-liter formula in 1967, which had prompted Ferrari to create the Dino road models in memory of his son—the champion of the V6 engine family. The 166 F2's only outing in 1967 ended in retirement for Jonathan Williams, but in 1968 they contested every round with a driver squad that included Amon, Jacky Ickx, Brian Redman, Derek Bell, Brambilla, and others, and which, in spite of the formula now being dominated by the Cosworth-Ford-engined entries, did bring five hard-fought wins.

Although Ferrari was about to turn his back yet again on Formula Two and its southern hemisphere spin-offs as the 1970s forced him to concentrate on regaining Formula One form, these varied activities show that there has usually been more to Ferrari than was ever likely to hit the popular headlines.

Formula One Dreams (and Nightmares)

In 1950, the governing body of motor sport, the FIA, created an official World Championship of Drivers and an International Cup for Formula One Manufacturers. Those were the modern successors to the more complicated structure of Grand Prix racing immediately before World War Two, when the nearest thing to a world champion was the committee-nominated "Champion of Europe." As before, there would still be Grands Prix which qualified for the championship (also called Grande Epreuves) and races called Grands Prix which didn't, and they might be for anything from Formula One models to Formula Two, even sportscars.

Either way, when the "modern" world championship was created in 1950, Ferrari was there. Fifty-two years later it is still there. Ferrari has disputed every championship in the series, and in that alone it is unique among all Grand Prix manufacturers. But other aspects mark Ferrari out: it has always built its own engines and transmissions as well as its own chassis; even when commercial sponsorship became inevitable Ferrari never completely gave up the traditional red racing colors of Italy; and however bad things sometimes looked, its support never wavered.

The hardware

Given his long history with the Alfa Romeo Grand Prix team between the wars, there was never much doubt that, once he had launched his own designs, Enzo Ferrari would aim for the highest rank, and that's exactly what he did right from the very start. When he created his first machine, the 1.5-liter V12-engined 125, the exotic and complex design was obviously conceived for maximum performance. But just as significantly, the 1.5-liter capacity was no coincidence either. When Gioacchino Colombo was laying down that first classic Ferrari engine design, the new "Formula One," as the premier racing category came to be known after the war, was for

Previous page *Ferrari pit stop practice, 1999*

Right *Villoresi's Ferrari 125 F1 in the paddock at the 1950 Swiss Grand Prix*

Above *1949/51 Ferrari 125/166 America, here driven by John Surtees at Goodwood, 1997*

engines of 4.5 liters without a supercharger, or 1.5 liters with. While some of his rivals had the luxury of being able to build big engines for Formula One and smaller ones for sportscars to run under different regulations, Ferrari couldn't yet extend his limited resources that far. So he started with adaptability.

But that did not mean that he started with compromise. Compared with almost any direct rival, the original Ferrari V12 was already one of the most technically advanced engines in the world, and once a supercharger had been added, it was every inch a Grand Prix engine—not the most powerful in the world, but certainly no also-ran.

At first, in fact, Ferrari's chassis were rather less suited to the Formula One role than the engines, and in the earliest days the weakest link was often the transmission. But Ferrari's Grand Prix racing career had to start somewhere, and his intentions were signaled by the fact that when he launched the 125, he promised a range of Sport, Competition, and Grand Prix versions. After the first Ferraris had cut their teeth in several lesser races bearing the title "Grand Prix," in 1948 Ferrari began Formula One Grand Prix racing proper.

In September of that year Ferrari unveiled the Grand Prix version of his 125, the 125 GP. For its very first single-seater outings, the 125 had been a two-seater reduced to one seat, with the driver on the right-hand side and the passenger space smoothly faired over with a solid tonneau. It was stripped of all the equipment that made the original 125 a sportscar, including the cycle wings, the lights, passenger windscreen, and absolutely any surplus weight that could be thrown out. But the fact was it was still a sportscar adapted for single-seater racing, not a true single-seater. The 125 GP, Ferrari's first purpose-built Formula One machine, changed all that.

It was a big step forwards. Like the 125 Sports, the 125 GP had a five-speed manual transmission in unit with the engine, and both sat in a fairly simple cross-braced oval-tube

Above *1949 Ferrari 125 F1 engine, shown here in the first "Thin Wall" special, with two-stage supercharging*

frame; it had independent front suspension with double control arms and a transverse leaf spring. Unlike the two-seaters it had independent rear suspension via semi-trailing arms and swing axles, first with torsion bars, then with a transverse leaf spring (rather than the rigid axle on longitudinal leaf springs of the 125 Sports models). It still had drum brakes all round, but they were upgraded—and, of course, for Formula One the 1.5-liter V12, although originally still only using one camshaft per cylinder bank, was supercharged to give around 230bhp compared with the 120bhp or so of the 1.5-liter engine in its most powerful, unblown 125 sportscar form.

The early races

This was the design Ferrari first wheeled out, even before the creation of the official world championship, for the Italian Grand Prix in September 1948 on a circuit in the Valentino Park in Turin. He entered three virtually identical machines, for Raymond Sommer (who had been closely involved alongside Colombo in the development of the 125 engine), Giuseppe Farina, and Prince Bira of Siam. It was a promising debut. Sommer put the quickest of the 125 GPs on the front row of the grid and took an encouraging third place in wet and slippery conditions, behind Jean-Pierre Wimille's Alfa Romeo 158 and Luigi Villoresi's Maserati. His two team-mates failed to finish, Farina having crashed and Bira suffering a broken transmission. The next time out, at Lake Garda, Farina gave the 125 GP its first win, but that was the high spot of the team's first season. At the last race, the Monza Grand Prix, neither of the two 125 GPs entered finished, Farina's because the transmission was sick, Sommer's because the driver was. Still, it hadn't been a bad single-seater debut year.

Ferrari's fortunes were definitely on the up. In 1949, the year before the championship proper got under way, they started with a mildly uprated version of the 125 GP for the Belgian Grand Prix at Spa Francorchamps, where Villoresi and Alberto Ascari opened the scoring with

Above *1951, Ascari and Farina line up at the wheels of two Ferrari 375s, Pescara. This is a very rare color photograph from this period.*

second and third places behind Louis Rosier's unsupercharged 4.5 Talbot, which had gone through the race without a gas stop (the supercharged Ferraris couldn't do that). Fourth place fell to a 125 GP, too, one of two "customer" entries Ferrari had sold, in this case to English driver Peter Whitehead. The other 125 GP sale, incidentally, was to British industrialist Tony Vandervell, the manufacturer of "thin wall" engine bearings. With his own product in the engine, plus a number of other modifications and a coat of British Racing Green paint, this design became the first of a number of "Thin Wall Specials" which in turn laid the foundations for the championship-winning Vanwall Grand Prix models.

Ferrari, meanwhile, enjoyed growing success through the rest of 1949, with wins in the Swiss and Czech Grands Prix (Ascari first with Villoresi second in Berne; Whitehead in his own machine winning in Czechoslovakia). They also won the Grand Prix of Europe at Monza (Ascari again), the Dutch Grand Prix (Villoresi) and the non-championship but very prestigious Daily Express Trophy race at Silverstone (Ascari).

Then came 1950, the first year of the new world championship. Ferrari had a new design, which had actually appeared late in 1949, at the Italian Grand Prix in September. It was labeled the 125 F1 and was a development of the 125 GP, with more power in a better chassis. The camshaft count was up from two to four, two-stage supercharging replaced single-stage, and power was up to around 290bhp. The wheelbase was longer, the tracks were wider, and this machine looked as graceful as its predecessor had looked dumpy. It was Ferrari's best so far, but unfortunately for them the Alfa Romeo 158 "Alfettas," the car Enzo had helped create before the

Right *Gonzalez brings his Ferrari 375 in to take first place at the British Grand Prix at Silverstone, 1951. This was Ferrari's first World Championship Grand Prix win and marked the end of the era of Alfa Romeo dominance*

Bottom right *Mike Hawthorn in the Ferrari 555 Super Squalo at the Spanish Grand Prix in Barcelona, 1954*

war, were better still. Alfa took the six-race championship with considerable ease, Giuseppe Farina becoming the first official world champion driver. The three races Farina didn't win, Alfa team-mate Juan Manuel Fangio did. Alfa's other driver, Luigi Fagioli, took third place in the championship with five second places.

The Ferrari team, headed by Ascari, Sommer, and Villoresi, couldn't get close to the Alfas in the world championship rounds, even when they uprated the 125 F1 with De Dion rear suspension. The best they had achieved by mid-season was second places in the non-championship races in Pau, San Remo, and the Grand Prix in Monaco, and for Enzo, second wasn't nearly good enough. He was ready to try another approach with the first of his non-supercharged 4.5-liter Formula One machines. The theory was that their broader spread of power should give them an edge on the tighter circuits, while better gas consumption should be an advantage everywhere. It was obvious that the supercharged Ferraris would never match the blown Alfettas for sheer speed.

Appropriately, the first unsupercharged Ferrari Formula One design, with its Lampredi-

designed V12, made its debut at Spa, where Talbot had previously shown Ferrari the benefit of good gas consumption. It started life, driven by Ascari, as a "275 F1" with a capacity of only 3.3 liters, but by September's Italian Grand Prix it had grown to the full 4.5 and the definitive type number 375 F1. That still wasn't enough to catch the flying Alfas, of course, but it was good enough to round the season off with another second place, and at least it had started Ferrari in a new direction for the future.

The 375 actually scored its first win before the end of 1950, in the non-championship end-of-season race in Barcelona, where Ascari and Dorino Serafini (in his only Ferrari Formula One race) finished first and second, with Villoresi third in a 4.1-liter interim model. But Alfa weren't there. Ferrari finally beat them the following year, Enzo noting the emotion of the moment: "when [José Froilán] Gonzalez, at the wheel of a Ferrari, left 159 and the whole of the Alfa team behind him, for the first time in a direct confrontation with us, I cried for joy." It wasn't quite, as Ferrari suggested, the first time that the two great rivals had raced head-to-head that year, and it wasn't even the first time Ferrari had won in 1951. They did that courtesy of Villoresi in the opening, non-championship race in Syracuse, but as in Barcelona in 1950, Alfa weren't there. Nor were they at Pau or San Remo, where Ferrari continued to win, first with Villoresi then Ascari, but those weren't championship races either, so the real showdown was still to come.

The two teams did race against each other in the Swiss Grand Prix, where Piero Taruffi snatched second place as both Ascari (recovering from burns) and Villoresi struggled, but Fangio kept the Alfa flag flying by winning the race. They met again in the Belgian Grand Prix, where Ascari and Villoresi were second and third to Farina's Alfetta, and they raced head-to-head at the French Grand Prix, where Gonzalez, the "Pampas Bull" from Argentina, took Taruffi's place but handed his drive over to Ascari, who finished second to Fangio's Alfa (which had also been shared, with Fagioli).

Then, in July at Silverstone, the showdown as Ferrari interpreted it happened, and Gonzalez won. He was fastest in practice, disputed the lead throughout the race, and took full advantage of the unblown Ferrari's non-stop fuel capability to beat Fangio and the leading Alfa into second place, with Villoresi's Ferrari third. It would be the first of three championship wins for Ferrari

Bottom left *Hawthorn kicks up some dust at Aintree 1955, in Ferrari 625 F1*

Bottom right *1954 Ferrari 625 F1 engine*

Above Fangio in the Ferrari D50, on his way to winning British Grand Prix at Silverstone, and the 1956 world championship

that year and, as it turned out, it would be the beginning of the end of an era. Ascari gave Ferrari victory in both Germany and Italy, but Alfa narrowly kept the title, Fangio six points ahead of Ascari.

At the end of the year, with another championship comprehensively won, Ferrari's main rival announced that they were withdrawing from Grand Prix racing, which in turn prompted the FIA, faced with the prospect of no serious challengers for Ferrari, to decide that the 1952 championship would be Formula Two. The outcome of that, as previously described, was two successive championship years for Ferrari with Ascari in the four-cylinder 500 F2, which swept all before it. In 1952 he won six times and Taruffi won once; in 1953 he won five more, while Hawthorn and Farina added one Grand Prix each, as the 500 F2 proved uncatchable.

Formula One revisited

For 1954 the world championship reverted to Formula One, but a new Formula One, for unsupercharged machines of 2.5 liters—and that was close enough to the old Formula Two to suggest that Ferrari might be the team to beat. The problem, though, was that the two-year break had given other manufacturers a certain amount of development time, and although Alfa had gone, Ferrari now faced another serious Italian rival in Maserati. Before the year was out they also found themselves facing an even more formidable foe: Mercedes Benz, returning to Grand Prix racing for the first time since the pre-war days of the legendary, state-backed Silver Arrows.

By the end of the year, the drivers' champion was Juan Manuel Fangio, and he had won with both Maserati and Mercedes. In Argentina and Belgium he drove the Italian car, the 250F, and won both races; for the rest of the season he switched to the German W196 and won another four, in France, Germany, Switzerland, and Italy.

Ferrari struggled. Following the lead of the Formula Two success, their 1954 Grand Prix armory was headed by a four-cylinder model, the 2.5-liter 625 F1 developed from the previous year's ultra-successful Formula Two chassis. But they had another string to their 1954 Formula One bow, the 553 F1 "Squalo." Like the 625 it had four-cylinder 2.5-liter power and Formula Two links—in this case having been developed from the space-framed 553 F2 of 1953—and like that automobile it had taken its nickname ("squalo" means "shark") from the shape of its bulbous side tanks. Their 1954 driver line-up included Farina, Gonzalez, Hawthorn, and Frenchman Maurice Trintignant, among others, but only Gonzalez and Hawthorn won Grands Prix for Ferrari that year, in Britain and Spain respectively.

It was Fangio's second title, and he notched up his third in 1955, staying with Mercedes to win another four Grands Prix out of the six-race series. His team-mate Stirling Moss won the British Grand Prix, and with Ferrari mainly relying on the under-achieving 553 Squalo but still occasionally racing the outdated 625, only Trintignant prevented a Mercedes clean sweep and avoided a blank Ferrari scoresheet by winning in Monaco after both Mercedes' star drivers had retired. By that time Ferrari had created what they called the 555 Supersqualo, but it was actually the old-faithful 625 that hung on to win in Monte Carlo.

For 1956, everything had changed, and very much in Ferrari's favor. After being at the center of the 1955 Le Mans tragedy which killed their driver Pierre Levegh and some 85 spectators, at the end of the season Mercedes withdrew from racing again (as they might have done anyway, with nothing left to prove). Maserati, with the simple but brilliantly effective 250F, would still be a threat, but Ferrari had a new ace up their sleeves: Juan Manuel Fangio. With three world championships already won, the Argentine superstar stepped into the Ferrari seat made vacant by the retirement of 1950 champion Farina, alongside (among others) Luigi Musso and Englishman Peter Collins.

And that wasn't the only dramatic change. For the last couple of years, Lancia had been the third major Italian marque in Grand Prix racing, having tasted a degree of success with the V8-engined D50 single-seaters with their distinctive pannier gas tanks. But by 1956 Lancia had lost their star driver Ascari, who had been killed testing a Ferrari sportscar at Monza in the summer of 1955, and they were in major financial trouble. The racing team was disbanded as a result and the vehicles were sold to Ferrari, who would run them as Lancia-Ferraris through 1956 and 1957. Part of the deal, organized by the Italian Automobile Club, was a five-year grant to Ferrari from Lancia's (and Ferrari's) future owners, Fiat—a forerunner, in a way, of Fiat's later sponsorship of the Ferrari team.

It turned out to be a fine partnership all round as Fangio in the Ferrari-developed D50 won his fourth championship, and Ferrari's third. He won the Argentine Grand Prix sharing Musso's machine, and the British and German Grands Prix, while his impressive team-mate Collins won in Belgium and France to harry him for the title, although in the end the two were split by Stirling Moss, who had been simply brilliant in his privately entered Maserati.

Then, unexpectedly, in 1957 the bubble burst and Ferrari didn't win a single Grand Prix. By now the D50s were far more Ferrari than Lancia, but that year they just didn't work. Fangio, having returned to Maserati, took the championship back to Ferrari's old rivals, and it has to be said that he deserved his fourth title in a row. The 250F was no longer the fastest entry by right, and Fangio's wins included what he reckoned his finest victory ever, when he overtook the Ferraris of Hawthorn and Collins to score a legendary win on the old Nurburgring.

Above *Mike Hawthorn at Spa in the 1958 Ferrari Dino 246 F1. He would go on to win the world championship*

Right *Monaco 1962, Phil Hill driving the "shark-nose" Ferrari 156*

Below *John Surtees at Monaco in 1963 Ferrari 156*

For Ferrari it was a one-year blip. In 1958 they were champions again with Collins' great friend Mike Hawthorn, who became Britain's first Grand Prix world champion even though he won only one Grand Prix, in France. After the Lancia interlude, the cars were pure Ferrari again. In fact, 1958 saw the start of one of their great lines in the V6-engined Dino 246 F1, designed by Vittorio Jano along the lines apparently suggested by Dino Ferrari. Whatever the extent of Dino's real involvement before his death in 1956, these first front-engined Dinos really were superb Grand Prix designs. Moss actually scored four wins in 1958 (with Cooper, then Vanwall) and might have wondered about the championship scoring system, but the fact was that Hawthorn backed up his single win with five seconds and a third, while Moss added just one second and five retirements. It might not have been the most exciting way to win a drivers' championship—Vanwall beat Ferrari to the manufacturers' title—but the sheer consistency of Hawthorn and the 246 F1 was remarkable.

There was a downside, though. Peter Collins, having proved capable of running with the best of them on his day, and having won the British Grand Prix at Silverstone for Ferrari, was killed during the German Grand Prix at the Nurburgring. Hawthorn, his best friend, made up his mind there and then to retire at the end of the year, and he did so. But in January 1959, just months after he had taken the title, he too was killed, in a road accident in England.

All this affected the surprisingly sentimental Enzo Ferrari quite badly, but the business of racing had to go on, and in 1959 the team regrouped, with a revised design, the 256 F1, and a new driver line-up—although that was something Ferrari juggled quite extensively. In seven races he used no fewer than seven drivers: Britons Tony Brooks and Cliff Allison, Americans Phil Hill and Dan Gurney, Frenchman Jean Behra, Belgian Olivier Gendebien, and German aristocrat Count Wolfgang "Taffy" von Trips. This cosmopolitan crowd, however, scored just two wins between them (both by Brooks, in France and Germany) while the British Coopers began to show that mid-engines were likely to be the way forward. And for the first time in a decade Ferrari missed one Grand Prix altogether, pulling out of the British race after industrial strikes in Italy.

Above left *John Surtees at Monaco in 1964 Ferrari 158*

Above *Monza, John Surtees in 1965 Ferrari 158*

The rear-engined Dino

The year 1960 was when most of the rest of the industry was edging towards rear engines, though Ferrari appeared to be stubbornly resisting it. If he had an excuse at all it was that this was the last year of the 2.5-liter Formula One and a more appropriate time to make the big change would be the start of the new 1.5-liter formula in 1961, but really he was just being Enzo Ferrari. He did, in fact, construct a mid-engined 2.5-liter model, also numbered 246 Dino, but it ran only once, in Monaco. For the rest of the year Ferrari relied on the latest version of the front-engined 256 F1. That helped restrict the team to just one 1960 win, for Phil Hill at Monza, and with not much more than a second for Allison in Argentina and a third for Hill in Monaco it was one of Ferrari's sparsest years for a long time. They didn't even enter for the US Grand Prix.

At Ferrari, though, as always, things rarely stood still for long. While the now mainly British opposition hoped that the start of the 1.5-liter formula might be delayed to give them more time to acquire the right engines, Ferrari quietly got on with creating what was undoubtedly the best engine for the start of the 1961 season, the new 1.5-liter V6 Dino. What's more, he put it behind the driver, in one of the prettiest cars he'd ever made—the "shark-nose" 156.

Once Stirling Moss had driven the race of his life (or at least one of them) to win the Monaco Grand Prix in Rob Walker's privately entered and decidedly underpowered Cooper, the Ferraris dominated the season. The sheer genius of Moss won again in a Lotus at the Nurburgring, and Ferrari missed the US Grand Prix for the second time (leaving Innes Ireland to score the first win for the works Lotus team), but won everything else. Giancarlo Baghetti won in France, von Trips in Holland and Great Britain, Hill in Belgium and Italy. At Monza, Hill clinched the world championship, having disputed it all season with von Trips, but he won in the most tragic circumstances. Going into this race von Trips was actually leading the championship, but on only his second lap he made contact with Jim Clark's Lotus. Both machines crashed, von Trips' Ferrari taking off into the crowd, killing the driver and fourteen spectators. Ferrari decided not to stop his other drivers and Hill won the race, and with it the championship, by a single point from his dead team-mate. Ferrari also secured the constructors' title, but it was a terrible and controversial way to finish a great season.

The team was now back on the switchback. In 1962, as the British manufacturers got fully into their stride, Ferrari stuck with the 156 and had another year with no wins at all, plus three more missed races: in France in mid-year, and in America and South Africa at season's end.

Their best results, from Hill, were one second place and a couple of thirds, but it was a season best forgotten, as Graham Hill's BRM confirmed the title over Jim Clark's Lotus by winning the last race. By that stage, of course, Ferrari weren't even also-rans, and they finished a lowly sixth in the constructors' league.

Surtees signs

Things weren't a great deal better in 1963, as Ferrari's new signing John Surtees, the former motor-cycle world champion and one of the few men successfully to make the move from two wheels to four at the very highest level, gave the team a single win, in Germany. That, though, was as much down to his skill as it was to the ability of the latest model, the fuel-injected 156 F1, which already had a more conventional, single-aperture nose shape, and towards the end of the season was completely redesigned around a unibody chassis.

That was the bridge to the following season's machine, and another peak after the latest trough. For 1964 Ferrari had two front-line drivers in Surtees and Lorenzo Bandini, and during the course of the season called on no fewer than three different designs: the V6-engined unibody 156, the V8-engined unibody 158, and, in a completely new direction, the flat-12-powered 512 F1. As well as his great driving skills, Surtees also brought to the team a level of technical understanding that was rare even among the best test drivers, and as such he contributed to all aspects of his 1964 world championship, but in the end he needed a bit of luck, too.

He had won in Germany and in Italy mid-season and had enough top-six finishes to give himself a slim chance of the championship as it went to the final round in Mexico, but he could only win if he finished well up and his two championship rivals, Graham Hill and Jim Clark, didn't. Surtees, still using the 158 V8 as he had all season, finished second to American Dan Gurney's Brabham. Clark had taken pole position and fastest lap, but his race was ruined by an engine oil leak and he finished fifth; Hill could only manage eleventh, having been hit by Surtees' Ferrari team-mate Bandini while he was in second place and heading for the title. Despite that, Surtees deserved his championship win, and so did Ferrari.

Below
top *Jackie Ickx in Ferrari 312, at the British Grand Prix 1970*
bottom *Clay Regazzoni in Ferrari 312 B/2, at the British Grand Prix 1971*

Into the wilderness

It was Surtees' one and only four-wheel Grand Prix title, and Ferrari's last for longer than they were used to. With the continued emergence of British Grand Prix teams such as Brabham, BRM, Cooper, and Lotus, all except BRM using the superb off-the-rack Coventry-Climax V8 engine, the Ferrari team had a lean time in the final year of the 1.5-liter formula and won nothing: Surtees and Bandini struggled to make the complex flat-12 512 F1 work and occasionally preferred to persevere with the older 158 V8. Ferrari wouldn't fare much better through the opening years of the new 3-liter formula, but characteristically they never gave up trying.

The 3-liter formula began in 1966, and Ferrari really ought to have been in the same position as they had been at the start of the 1.5-liter formula a few years before—ready to cruise to the championship while the rest were still getting their acts together. In fact, most of the others did run strictly interim engines, but it wasn't Ferrari who benefitted, it was Brabham. Their production-based Repco V8 was much less sophisticated than Ferrari's new 3-liter V12

Above left *Lauda on his way to winning the championship at Monaco in 1975 in the Ferrari 312 T and* ***right*** *close-up of cabin*

and shouldn't have been anywhere near as powerful, but it was definitely more reliable. For once, a relatively unsophisticated engine in a fairly simple but rugged design was the way to go, and Brabham took both the 1966 and 1967 championships, the first for Jack Brabham himself, the second for his tough-as-nails team-mate Denny Hulme.

For Ferrari, they were miserable years indeed. Having helped develop the new 312 for the beginning of the new formula, Surtees drove just two races at the start of 1966 before having a major row with Enzo (over Le Mans) and walking out to join Cooper, who were briefly using Maserati engines. He'd won his last race for the prancing horse in Belgium, and Ferrari undoubtedly missed him—though Enzo, of course, would never admit such a thing. Later in the year Mike Parkes and Ludovico Scarfiotti raced alongside Bandini, and Scarfiotti gave the team something to cheer about by winning the best race he could have won, the Italian Grand Prix at Monza, in front of hundreds of thousands of screaming fans. But Ferrari missed two races again: in Britain, because of more strikes in the Italian motor industry; and in Mexico, because the last race of the year was hardly likely to rescue his season anyway.

In almost every respect, 1967 was even worse. The team scored no wins at all and Bandini was killed early in the season in a dreadful, fiery accident on the harbor front at Monaco when he couldn't immediately be released from his blazing machine. Chris Amon gave them a few third places, but it was a season to forget.

In 1968, Ferrari at least got back on to the winners' podium as Jacky Ickx won the French Grand Prix with the improving 312 F1. But now, winning was going to be tougher than ever, at least for a while, as the brilliant new Ford-financed Cosworth V8—an off-the-rack engine which in the right chassis was the class of the field—started to change the face of Grand Prix racing.

Indeed, for the next few years Ferrari picked up mainly crumbs, albeit in the familiar up–down pattern. A desperate 1969 and a rock-bottom sixth place in the constructors' championship was followed by a "nearly" year when Ickx won three Grands Prix (Austria, Canada, and Mexico) to take the runner-up spot in the drivers' championship behind Jochen Rindt. Clay Regazzoni won another with the much more effective 312 B, putting Ferrari back to second in the constructors' table. Then Ferrari recorded just three wins over the next three years: Mario Andretti (who certainly pleased the fans) in South Africa and Holland in 1971; and Ickx—the six-times Le Mans winner who so often seemed to be on the brink of winning the

Above *Niki Lauda at speed in Ferrari 312 T2, Monaco 1977. Lauda came second in the race and was on his way to winning his second championship*

ultimate Formula One prize but never quite pulled it off—in Germany in 1972. And Andretti and Ickx weren't the only high-fliers who were finding life with Ferrari tough during this bad patch: Amon, Pedro Rodriguez, and Arturo Merzario all struggled. Ferrari struggled, period.

Lauda revives Ferrari

The odd thing about this slump, for anyone who wasn't Ferrari, was that the team's reputation never went through the floor. It was tarnished, certainly, but it was hard to find anyone who didn't, deep down, reckon that Ferrari had the strength to fight back. Certainly the light at the end of the tunnel looked brighter in 1974, when Ferrari took three wins. Regazzoni scored in Germany, and the other two came from a very important new boy, one Niki Lauda.

Lauda had clawed his way to the top of the motor racing ladder by mortgaging everything he owned and borrowing everything he could borrow. He had the same commitment on the track as he displayed off it, and he was good. He finished second in his first Grand Prix for Ferrari, in Argentina in 1974, and won his fourth, in Spain. Regazzoni was runner-up in the championship, just three points adrift of McLaren's Emerson Fittipaldi, but Lauda was the man of the moment. It was the start of a partnership which would eventually see him overtake Ascari's long-standing record of thirteen wins for the prancing horse, and Lauda's record of fifteen would stand just as long, before Michael Schumacher comprehensively overtook it at the turn of the century.

Lauda didn't just give Ferrari race wins, he gave them something much more important:

***Above** Jody Scheckter in the Ferrari 312 T4 at the Spanish Grand Prix, on his way to winning the 1979 title*

more championships. Ferrari gave him the machinery to do the job with a series of wonderful-looking and obviously fairly effective new designs, the 312 T and 312 T2, with their transverse transmissions and bucketsful of flat-12 power. Lauda used them to the absolute limits, and in 1975 and 1977 he won the world title against the toughest of opposition. He won five Grands Prix in 1975—in Monaco, Belgium, Switzerland, France, and the USA—while Regazzoni added a win in Italy, a bonus for the home crowd. In 1977 Lauda won "only" three races, South Africa, Germany, and Holland, while new team-mate Carlos Reutemann won in Brazil. But in many ways, Lauda's 1977 title was even more impressive than 1975.

The fact that he was alive at all was remarkable, and the fact that he was world champion again was little short of a miracle. A year before, Lauda's world had been stood on its head. In the German Grand Prix at the Nurburgring in 1976 he had a huge accident on his second lap and was pulled from a blazing wreck, badly burned, by other drivers who had stopped to help. In hospital he was so near death that he was given the last rites. Having racked up five Grand Prix wins before the accident—in Brazil, South Africa, Belgium, Monaco, and Great Britain—he was still in the championship race against McLaren's James Hunt, and incredibly he was back racing within a few weeks, even though he was still in terrible pain and scarred for life. At Monza for the Italian Grand Prix, almost unbelievably, he was back in the points with fourth place. He took third in the USA, and went to the final race of the season, in Japan, three points ahead of Hunt.

The weather at the Mount Fuji circuit was appalling, and as Mario Andretti splashed to victory for Lotus, Lauda pulled out of the race after just a couple of laps, saying that it was too dangerous to carry on. Far from being a cop-out, it was one of the most courageous decisions he

***Above right** Gilles Villeneuve driving to win the 1981 Monaco Grand Prix in the Ferrari 126 CK*

***Above** Villeneuve sitting in the pits, showing a car with much of the body off*

***Below** 1985 Ferrari F1/156 V6 turbo*

ever made. As Lauda watched, Hunt clawed his way to fourth place, to win the championship by a single point. Lauda had no regrets, and that made him a very special man even by Ferrari standards, and when, still only barely recovered from his injuries, he gave the Maranello team that next world title in 1977, he guaranteed his place as one of their best-loved sons.

Again, though, it was good news before bad for Ferrari, and at the end of the season Lauda went off to join Brabham, now powered by Ferrari's old adversary Alfa Romeo. Ferrari's new drivers for 1978 were Reutemann and an extremely impressive rookie, Gilles Villeneuve. They took five wins between them, but it wasn't enough as Andretti (still with Lotus) took six for himself to secure the drivers' and constructors' championships. Reutemann's wins in Brazil, Britain, and at both US Grands Prix (east and west) helped him to third place in the championship (and Ferrari to a distant second). Villeneuve's season, capped by his first win in the final round in his native Canada, marked him out as one of the most spectacularly aggressive new talents in years. He looked like a champion in the making, and became an instant hero to Ferrari fans.

But it wasn't Villeneuve who gave Ferrari their third title in five years, it was his new team-mate for the 1979 season, South African Jody Scheckter. Scheckter had already had a third place in the drivers' championship in 1976, with Tyrrell, and a runner-up spot in 1977, with Wolf. In 1979, with Ferrari, he won. He was never as spectacular as Villeneuve, and the pair won three races each (Scheckter in Belgium, Monaco, and Italy, Villeneuve in South Africa and at both US races), but the minor placings gave Scheckter the championship with Villeneuve four points adrift. And, of course, Ferrari were conclusive winners of the constructors' cup.

Back to the wilderness again

After that it all started to go strangely wrong. After Scheckter's win, it would be 21 years before Ferrari took the drivers' championship again, and there were times during that period when Ferrari struggled harder, and for longer, than they had ever done before.

In 1980, with the 312 "transversale" series of designs now up to 312 T5, Scheckter's and Villeneuve's best results were three fifth places between them. Only Alfa scored fewer points in the constructors' series, where Ferrari finished a miserable tenth. A fifth place in 1981, when Ferrari joined the ranks of the turbocharged Grand Prix runners with the powerful but almost undrivable 126 CK, was only marginally better, but Villeneuve did at least manage a couple of spectacular wins, in Monaco and Spain.

Then came 1982, and one of the most harrowing seasons Ferrari had ever known. Before the Belgian Grand Prix in May, Villeneuve had scored one second place, in the San Marino Grand Prix at Imola where Didier Pironi had won after apparently ignoring team orders not to overtake his team-mate. The two drivers never spoke again, and two weeks later Villeneuve was dead, killed in a freak practice accident at Zolder after hitting another car.

It was a particularly low spot for Enzo Ferrari, because of all the great drivers he had ever had, Enzo believed Villeneuve was among the greatest, not only for his speed but for his passion. There were even people who thought that Villeneuve had become like a son to Ferrari. No one could really take his place, but from the Dutch Grand Prix onwards, after three races for which Ferrari had just a single entry for Pironi, a second machine was brought out for the amiable and able Frenchman Patrick Tambay. Pironi won that race, but in another tragic episode for Ferrari he was terribly injured in a practice accident during the German Grand Prix at Hockenheim and was very lucky to survive. It was an even more emotional moment, therefore, when Tambay won the race, lifting the team's spirits at least a little.

The rest of 1982 was really going through the motions for Ferrari. Andretti rejoined for two of the last three races, but when the 1983 season began the driver line-up was an all-French affair, Tambay alongside René Arnoux, and a fine pair they made. In a hugely competitive season Nelson Piquet ultimately won the drivers' title for Brabham BMW, but with strong third and fourth places, Arnoux (with wins in Canada, Germany, and Holland) and Tambay (with a single win, in San Marino) gave Ferrari another constructors' cup.

But the rot had not yet been fully treated, at least by Ferrari's better standards. The final year of the 126 family was 1984, with the 126 C4, and the high spot was a lone win for rookie Michele Alboreto in the Belgian Grand Prix. Although his efforts with Arnoux gave Ferrari a constructors' runner-up spot, they had way fewer than half the points of runaway winners McLaren.

This state of affairs was now more of a pattern than a glitch. A new line started in 1985 with the 156-85, which became the F1-86 in 1986 and subsequently the F1-87, -88, -89, and so on into the early 1990s. After that, the F92A appeared for 1992, then a string of several different numbers: 412 T1B in 1994, 412 T2 in 1995, F310 in 1996, F10B in 1997, F300 in 1998, F399 in 1999, F1-2000 in 2000, and F1-2001 in 2001. However complicated this numbering system was, Ferrari's ups and downs in the closing years of the twentieth century were even more complex.

For the first of that list of cars, at least, results were hard to come by. Alboreto won in Canada and Germany in 1985, Arnoux won nothing—though he didn't have much opportunity to win: after finishing fourth in the Brazilian Grand Prix he left the team "by mutual agreement" and was replaced by Stefan Johansson, who stayed for the rest of the season, and for 1986. Amazingly, that still helped both Alboreto and Ferrari to second places in their respective championships. The following season was another win-free year for Ferrari. Johansson had a better time of it than Alboreto, but with just 37 points between them from sixteen races that wasn't saying much. In 1987, the musical chairs game for the second Ferrari saw Johansson

Above *1987 Monaco: Michele Alboreto follows Gerhard Berger driving Ferrari F1-87s*

Below *Nigel Mansell in the 1989 Ferrari F1-89 in Brazil*

Above *Alain Prost at the French Grand Prix 1990, driving the Ferrari 641 to the team's 100th Grand Prix victory. Prost won five races in the season, but that wasn't enough to claim the title*

replaced by Gerhard Berger, who gave the fans something to cheer with two fine wins, but not until the very end of the year, in Japan and Australia, by which time the Williams–Honda partnership of Piquet and Nigel Mansell had taken the constructors' championship by storm, and the first two places in the drivers' series.

Mansell's performances clearly weren't overlooked by Ferrari, and after an unchanged driver line-up for 1988 netted just one win for Berger, fortunately in Italy, Ferrari signed the fast but not always consistent Briton for 1989. He was a fine partner for Berger and they took as many wins that season as Ferrari had had in the three years from 1986 to 1988. Only three, it has to be admitted, but Mansell's high profile in particular made his two wins in Brazil and Hungary incredibly popular, and Berger added victory in Portugal.

Mansell won in Estoril the following season, but otherwise was overshadowed by his new team-mate, Alain Prost, the spectacularly quick but rather quiet superstar who was nicknamed "The Professor" for his ability to win by being cleverest, not just by being fastest. That talent helped him win five Grands Prix for Ferrari in 1990, including the team's 100th Grand Prix victory, in France. He also won in Brazil, Mexico, Britain, and Spain—but amazingly that wasn't enough to add another world title to the three he had already won with McLaren. Although he would add to that tally by winning for Williams in 1993, 1990 was the closest he ever came with Ferrari, and he left them at the end of 1991 without having scored another victory.

Times continued to be tough throughout 1991, and in 1992 Mansell showed Ferrari that they hadn't been wrong about his talent when he won the championship with a record number of wins in a single season—unfortunately, though, by now he was driving for Williams. Ferrari's pairing of Jean Alesi and Ivan Capelli, who was replaced at the end of the season by test driver Nicola Larini, not only didn't win a race, they scored just 21 points between them. That didn't look too good alongside Williams's aggregate of 164.

Alesi partnered Berger in 1993 for another win-free season, the team's first ever no-win hat trick. After a dreadful year for the sport which saw both Ayrton Senna and Roland Ratzenberger killed at Imola, Berger lightened the gloom for Ferrari in 1994 by winning in Germany, but it proved to be a one-off, as was Alesi's unexpected win in Canada in 1995. Podium finishes were few and far between.

A new era

Looking back, 1996 was finally the start of a real revival, and it was centered on one brilliant driver, Michael Schumacher. There would be huge contributions from the team around him, too—team principal Jean Todt, technical director Ross Brawn, and not least Ferrari boss Luca di Montezemolo, who kept backing the team even when everything looked lost, and owners Fiat, who kept funding it—but Schumacher was the star.

He was already a double world champion when he joined Ferrari, having secured back-to-back titles with Benetton in 1994 and 1995. If his ways of winning could sometimes be controversial, there was absolutely no question about his total commitment. That, as much as anything else, was what ultimately put Ferrari back on top of the ladder. The brilliant German not only brought the talent to drive, but also the personality to motivate the team as they hadn't been motivated in far too many years. The fans loved him, the team loved him. The press didn't always understand him, but Schumacher delivered. It still took time, though, and more than a bit of nerve-jangling frustration, and there was a brief stage when it looked as though it might

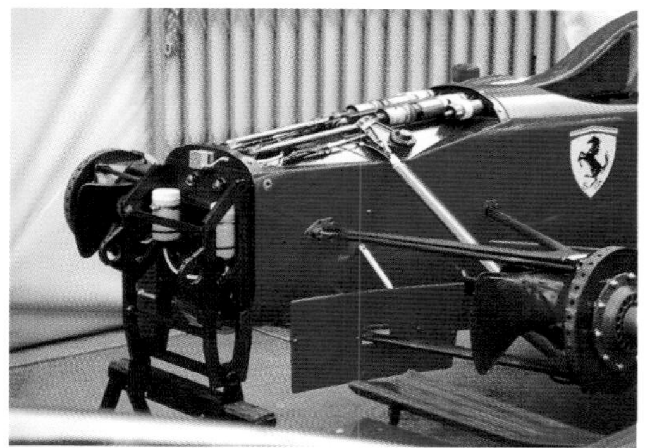

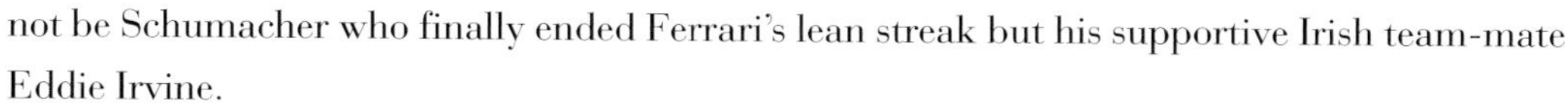

not be Schumacher who finally ended Ferrari's lean streak but his supportive Irish team-mate Eddie Irvine.

But back to 1996 and Schumacher's first season. After his astonishing success with Benetton, he came down to earth with his new employers, though he won three races, in Spain, Belgium, and Italy, to help Ferrari to second place in the constructors' championship. The fans, as well as the sponsors, had expected more, but even the remarkable partnership of Ferrari and Schumacher couldn't deliver miracles.

They were getting there, though, and in 1997 Schumacher disputed the title for the whole season with Jacques Villeneuve, son of Ferrari's late hero Gilles. Villeneuve, in the Williams–Renault, arguably had the better drive, but Schumacher was on a mission. He took brilliant wet-weather wins in Monaco and Belgium through sheer car control and fearsome commitment. He won in Canada, France, and Japan too, so, after a dramatic exchange of penalties which saw Schumacher reduced to sixth place in Austria and Villeneuve disqualified in France, the pair went to the last race, the European Grand Prix at Jerez, with the title on the line. In 1994, Schumacher had won the title after a controversial clash with Damon Hill in the last round, in Australia, which ended the Englishman's race and any chance of his taking the championship. In Jerez in 1997, Schumacher, whose Ferrari was clearly not as fast as Villeneuve's Williams, crashed out while attempting to hold him off for the lead. Villeneuve survived the clash, took third place and won the title. Schumacher was subsequently stripped of his runner-up position when the sports governing body decided he had made one aggressive move too many. But that wouldn't stop him being just as committed again.

In 1998, with six wins, Ferrari had another second place in the constructors' cup to show for another season of huge expectations and frustrating twists in the script. From the start of the season the McLarens dominated, but after two McLaren 1–2s, Schumacher won in Argentina. He had Coulthard to worry about too in the McLaren squad: in fact, both "second" drivers, Coulthard and Irvine, showed that they weren't there just to make up the numbers. Schumacher notched up a mid-season hat trick (Canada, France, Britain) to keep the championship alive,

***Top left** Schumacher drives the 1997 F310 to victory in the wet in Belgium*

***Above** Three views of the Ferrari pit at Monaco 1996*

Right *Schumacher on his way to winning the 2000 Japanese Grand Prix in the Ferrari F1 2000*

Above *Schumacher conducts the crowd from the Japanese Grand Prix podium after clinching the 2000 title*

Below *2001: Schumacher and Barichello make it a Ferrari 1–2 at the British Grand Prix, Silverstone*

Bottom right *September 2001, the Italian Grand prix at Monza. Ferrari ran their cars without showing sponsorship as a mark of respect for the events of September 11th. This is Barichello on his way to second place*

but he was always chasing from behind. He won again in Hungary, failed to finish after controversially hitting Coulthard in near zero visibility at an appallingly wet Spa, and after a suitably emotional win at Monza found himself tied on points with Hakkinen. A win for the Finn in the Luxembourg Grand Prix (held at the Nurburgring) sent him to the last round, at Suzuka in Japan, with a four-point lead. In a climax that would have sounded far-fetched as a film script, Schumacher stalled on the grid, had to start from last place, carved through into third place, closing gradually on leader Hakkinen, then suffered a blowout. Hakkinen won the race and the title. Schumacher settled again for second place.

The Flying Finn won again in 1999, and this time Schumacher could do even less about it as he spent half the season out of the car having badly broken his leg in a strange accident at the start of the British Grand Prix, where he ploughed almost head-on into a tire wall. Irvine had opened the season by winning in Australia, and Schumacher had won at Imola and in Monaco (with Irvine second), but with the German sidelined after Silverstone it was the Ulsterman who had to take the championship fight to the McLarens, supported for now by temporary team-mate Mika Salo. Irvine so nearly pulled off the impossible. He won in Austria, and at Hockenheim, where Salo waved him through under team orders. Then, with two rounds to go, Schumacher came back, for the first Malaysian Grand Prix. From pole position he settled into second place, deftly defending Irvine all the way to another win.

So the championship went to the wire yet again, and the last race was at Suzuka. There,

neither Schumacher nor Irvine could catch the inspired Hakkinen. "Schuey" came in second, Eddie third, just four points off the title he had looked so close to taking. The main consolation for Ferrari was that one part of the agony, at least, was over. For the first time since 1983 they were constructors' champions.

Finally, in 2000, Schumacher ended that seemingly eternal 21-year wait for the most prestigious title of all, the drivers' championship. Once again it was a straight fight between Schumacher and Hakkinen. Once again their respective team-mates—Coulthard, still at McLaren, and now Rubens Barrichello at Ferrari—were more than useful wild cards. This time Schumacher took the early lead with a hat trick in the first three races, in Australia, Brazil, and San Marino. Hakkinen fought back in Spain, then Schumacher won the European Grand Prix at the Nurburgring, and from there he pulled away. He had four worrying non-finishes in mid-season, but with wins in Canada, Italy, Japan, the USA, and Malaysia he was nineteen points ahead by season's end. This time Ferrari secured the double, drivers' and manufacturers' titles, and to make the year complete, Barrichello won in Germany and wept.

That is the sort of emotion Ferrari generates, even in its drivers, and there was more to come when Schumacher, again ably supported by Barrichello, made it a back-to-back double in 2001. Once again, the title chase was over before the end of the year. Nine more victories for Schumacher confirmed him as one of the greatest racing drivers of all time, Ferrari as the team you should never write off. Schumacher had crossed the finishing line first in Australia, Malaysia, Spain, Monaco, at the European Grand Prix, in France, Hungary, Belgium, and Japan; he had retired just twice, had five second places and a fourth. Barrichello added five seconds and four third places for a resounding constructors' win. It was as convincing a season as even Ferrari could have imagined. It made Schumacher the most prolific race winner in Grand Prix history, with 53 wins to Prost's previous record of 51, and it confirmed Ferrari as the team above all teams.

Ferrari have raced in more Grands Prix than any other team, more than seven hundred; they have won the most Grand Prix races, 147 of them; they hold the record for the most world championship points, the most pole positions, the highest number of fastest laps in Grands Prix. Probably most important of all to the team itself, Ferrari have won the most constructors' championships—eleven as of 2001. It's a record that's very hard to argue with.

Top *Schumacher, number 1 and* ***above*** *testing the Ferrari F2002 at Fiorano*

Bottom left *Barichello testing the F2002 in Barcelona*

GNF 97Y

Ferraris in All but Name

In the complicated world of motor sport, you can't always judge a book by its cover, especially where Ferrari is involved. According to the badges, the first Ferrari ever built wasn't a Ferrari, and over the years there have been many models that haven't strictly speaking been born under the sign of the prancing horse, but which nonetheless have Ferrari blood in their veins. We've told the story of the 815 by Auto Avio Costruzione, of the Dinos from Fiat and Ferrari, and of the Lancia Grand Prix cars Ferrari inherited in the 1950s. But those are only part of the Ferrari fringes, from the earliest days right through to the present, when not every Ferrari-engined machine on the Formula One grid is a Ferrari.

The fact is, Enzo Ferrari always did things exactly as they suited him—and whether the reasons were commercial or political, what sometimes suited him best was to hide behind other identities. That way he could enjoy the glory when things went right without suffering any serious embarrassment when things went wrong. To a degree, that still applies to Ferrari after Ferrari.

Nor did it apply only to the sporting side. Even beyond the Dinos, Ferrari once dabbled with road models that were Ferrari in all but name. This time it was all about image, and perhaps you could see Enzo's point. In the early 1960s, at a time when the Ferrari name was at one of its peaks, with Grand Prix and sportscar world championships still on the resumé and some of the greatest of Ferrari's big, front-engined GTs still crowning the production catalog, Ferrari had one of his less obvious ideas: to build a sub-1-liter GT in reasonable numbers for people who wouldn't otherwise be in the Ferrari marketplace. He developed the design, with a four-cylinder overhead-camshaft engine of just 850cc in a neat little two-door fastback body styled by Bertone, but he didn't have the resources to build or market it. Probably just as crucially, if he'd had problems putting Ferrari badges on the original mid-engined Dino, he would surely have been even more reluctant about putting them on a machine like this.

Which doesn't mean that the "Ferrarina," as it was nicknamed, was a bad design. It wasn't. For one thing, it was partly the work of Giotto Bizzarini, the great engineer whose work for Ferrari also included the legendary 250 GTO. There was a racing connection, too. The project was passed to another company, ASA, or Autocostruzione Società per Azioni, and among the

Previous page *1975 Lancia Stratos*

Below and right *1950/51 Thin Wall Special Number 3, the Ex Serafini Ferrari 375F1*

Left *The 1991 Minardi M192, Morbidelli at the wheel, San Marino Grnd Prix*

Below *1988-90 Lancia Thema 8.32*

backers of ASA were two of Ferrari's Grand Prix drivers, Giancarlo Baghetti and Lorenzo Bandini, who obviously took an interest in the development.

It went into production with capacity increased to just over one liter and claiming more than 95bhp—an extraordinary figure for such an engine in 1962, with or without a Ferrari badge. In this case, of course, it was strictly without, and while a lot of people might have paid a premium price for a small Ferrari, not many were standing in line to buy a small ASA rather than, say, a much cheaper Alfa or Abarth. Still, the project survived for around five years, and ASA built both coupés and a few convertibles, plus a couple of 1.5-liter six-cylinders, but probably fewer than a hundred vehicles in total.

Next of the Ferrari clones, beyond the Dinos but closely related, was essentially a competition entry with production connections, to satisfy the rule makers' production requirements in another class. This time, though, it wasn't for the race track, it was for the rally stage, and the machine was the fabulous Lancia Stratos, launched in 1972 after a couple of sneak previews in earlier Bertone show models.

By this stage, Lancia was owned by Fiat, and they saw a way to kick Lancia's struggling reputation back into life by attacking the world rally championship, with a version of the Dino V6 in a purpose-built mid-engined coupé. As with the Dino Formula Two models, the rules said it had to be based on a series-production unit, and just like Formula Two, it was. There was no problem with the engine, which had now been made in its thousands, and Lancia built enough copies of the Stratos to give them both a championship-winning rally design and a limited-production customer version for anyone who didn't mind a high price and a machine which was really far more suited to forest tracks than autostradas. As the world's first purpose-designed rallycar, it did exactly what it had been intended to do and put Lancia right back in the public eye, clocking up four Monte Carlo rally wins—the last of them as late as 1979, against a new breed of opposition—and three world championships through the mid-1970s.

It set a precedent for Ferrari-engined Lancias, too, including the Lancia–Ferrari sports racing prototypes described earlier and a next-generation Lancia rallycar, the hugely powerful turbocharged and supercharged mid-engined four-wheel-drive Delta S4, which was one of the fastest of all the Group B rally models (they were outlawed in the late 1980s because they were simply too quick for the sport's good). Lancia did another road version with Ferrari connections too, in the late 1980s, when a 32-valve Ferrari V8 under the hood of a mildly revised Thema sedan created the rather special 150mph Thema 8.32.

Right *The 2001 Prost car at Monanco*

Below *Monaco 1999, Sauber engineers work on the Petronas engine*

Away from the road and the rally stage, Ferrari's off-the-rack, and occasionally under-the-counter, contributions to the sharp end of motor sport have been numerous, if not always totally successful. The Thin Wall Specials were originally all-Ferrari, of course, but gradually became more Vandervell before the Vanwall proper was created. In the mid-1950s Briggs Cunningham switched from Chrysler Hemi V8 engines to Ferrari V12s in his Cunningham Le Mans designs. There were a few Cooper–Ferrari single-seaters on the fringes around 1960 too, before Ferrari himself committed fully to mid-engines, and over the years plenty of special builders have unofficially grafted Ferrari engines on to the most unlikely of high-powered racing hot-rods.

Much more recently Ferrari have also supplied versions of their Formula One prancing horse power on more formal terms to a few carefully chosen Grand Prix teams. Minardi ran Ferrari engines in Formula One in 1991, and Pierluigi Martini and Gianni Morbidelli took home half a dozen constructors' points. Dallara were Ferrari-powered for the next season, Martini following the engine and switching teams as Minardi turned to Ferrari's arch rival Lamborghini, who were making their only serious attack on Grand Prix racing. His team-mate was J. J. Lehto, but it was Martini who gave Dallara their only points, with two sixth places.

Best known among Ferrari engine users in the modern era, though, is undoubtedly Sauber, who started using "Petronas" V10s—supplied by Ferrari, and in effect the team's previous-season Formula One units—in 1997, since when they have worked their way further and further up the Grand Prix pecking order. In 2001 Prost, too, were Ferrari-powered, with the V10 engine labeled Acer, though for the team run by Ferrari's one-time star driver Ferrari power wasn't enough, even as Team Ferrari stormed to the title.

Which is maybe the most telling point of all. Enzo Ferrari always used to say that the engine was the most important part of the automobile, but however good it is, it isn't the only vital ingredient. Clearly, there are times when only a real Ferrari has the whole recipe.